Joan Stanley

is a graduate of Bennington College
in Vermont, and earned her D.Phil in Chinese Art History at
the University of Oxford. She has been studying various
aspects of Asian art since 1964 and spent four years studying
the arts of Japan *in situ*. Since 1991 she has been teaching at
National Tsing Hua University in Taiwan, where she is
Professor at the Center for General Education. Her books
include a study of Japanese reception and transformation of
Chinese literati painting, *The Transmission of Chinese Idealist
Painting to Japan: Notes on the Early Phase*, and a study of the
nature and function of forgeries in Chinese painting, *Old
Masters Repainted: Wu Zhen (1280-1354)
Prime Objects and Accretions.*

WORLD OF ART

This famous series
provides the widest available
range of illustrated books on art in all its aspects.
If you would like to receive a complete list
of titles in print please write to:
THAMES AND HUDSON
30 Bloomsbury Street, London WC1B 3QP
In the United States please write to:
THAMES AND HUDSON INC.
500 Fifth Avenue, New York, New York 10110

Printed in Singapore

JOAN STANLEY-BAKER

Japanese Art

with 167 illustrations, 20 in colour

THAMES AND HUDSON

© 1984 Thames and Hudson Ltd, London
Reprinted 1995

ISBN 0-500-20192-7

Printed and bound in Singapore by C.S. Graphics

Contents

Author's note

For clarity regarding their source, the names of monks, monasteries, artists and artworks originating in China are given in their Chinese form, while those of Japanese origin are given in Japanese. The Chinese suffix meaning temple, *-si*, appears as *-ji* in Japanese, and its Japanese equivalent is *-tera* or *-dera*: hence such names as Tōdaiji, Hōryūji, Wakakusadera.

Chinese words for painting, *hui* and *hua*, become *e* and *ga* in Japanese. They occur frequently as suffixes in words referring to styles or techniques, and are hyphenated only in the *-e* form to avoid ambiguity in reading: *onna-e, tsukuri-e,* etc. Special terms are capitalized only when preceded by proper names (eg *Kara-e*, Chinese-style painting; *Nihonga, Yamato-e*, Japanese-style painting); proper names functioning as verbs, however (eg japanization), are not capitalized, following such precedents as romanization or pasteurization.

CHAPTER ONE

Introduction

This book addresses itself to those who come to Japanese art for the first time, and introduces some of the most significant artistic innovations made on Japanese soil. The aim has not been to be comprehensive; certain major aspects of art and their traditions are not covered, major traditions which can best be seen in a fuller social context, such as Nō and Kabuki theatre, dance (some deriving from ancient Polynesian origins), and the tremendous achievements of swordsmiths and makers of miniatures. Those aspects which have been selected are intended to demonstrate the breadth and resilience of Japan's artistic spirit, which has withstood successive cultural inundations from the continent and emerged highly selective, adaptable, and always fully able to rediscover its own artistic roots.

Another purpose of the book is to identify those aspects of the Japanese spirit which were developed in art forms. Artists, especially up to the Muromachi period, were often working with, and transforming, apparently incompatible foreign ideas. This seems to me a greater challenge than the unhindered development of indigenous artistic traditions. To have continually taken and transformed diverse influences (whether from Korea, China, the South Seas, Europe or America) is a unique achievement. Japanese culture in general may be likened to an oyster, opening itself up to repeated onslaughts from the ocean and transforming grains of continental grit into pearls. These transformations obviously reflect Japanese preferences; but, more importantly, they indicate a particular kind of perception: it is possible to identify the patterns of adaptation which appear when Japanese art ingests new stimuli. Because they reflect cultural or ethnic traits, these patterns remain constant despite changing period-styles.

At the same time, the swing of the Japanese psychological pendulum seems wider than that of other peoples, and this is reflected in opposing tendencies in the arts. One tendency is to mirror the external world as it is perceived (direct imitation). A mirror is held up to the world, so to speak, and keeps outsiders from penetrating the essential delicacy and emotional

7

vulnerability of Japanese sensibility. Seeing in Japan a mirror-likeness of himself, the outsider loses interest and ceases to threaten.

The second tendency is introspective and insular, and fosters a creative urge to unparalleled delicacy and poetic imagery. Innate potentials, fully realized, gave birth to art forms and expressions unique to Japan. One is even tempted to propose that the subtlety, poignancy and sense of vulnerability in Japanese culture in general are protected from external disturbance and survive precisely by means of the public arts.

Examples of the first, mirror-image tendency, are the Asuka-Nara periods (when whole communities of continental artisans were imported), the late Kamakura and Muromachi periods (when Japanese artists were commissioned to work in Chinese styles), the Meiji period (when vast numbers of foreign experts, this time from Europe and North America, were imported to found schools of art, and when Japanese students were sent abroad in hundreds), and finally post-second-world-war Japan, whose art tries to be indistinguishable from Western models, in spite of the cultural and social differences between Tokyo or Osaka and New York, London or Paris. It is, however, the more introspective tendencies which best reveal Japanese uniqueness and ingenuity; the range includes the arts of Jōmon man, those of the Heian, Momoyama and early Edo periods.

It could be argued that in the absence of indigenous traditions and without artistic importations from abroad, throughout Japanese history, there would have been no ideas to work on, and no Japanese art at all. There are nevertheless distinct ways in which the Japanese have reacted to foreign stimuli. These are, on the one hand, a spontaneous identification with and rapid absorption of those new ideas which struck a responsive chord in the Japanese artist, and on the other, when required by self-conscious patrons, the mastery of styles and processes which might at first seem unbridgeably alien or mysterious. Given that most artistic processes and styles had to be imported, it may be suggested that the phases of introspection, when native traditions flourished, were times when artists enjoyed greater freedom in their selection and handling of styles, while the more assertive, outward-directed phases were times when the patrons' choices were conditioned by the prestige they might gain from mirroring some external style.

Non-Japanese viewers tend to respond more readily to the introspective phases (where the art is more characteristically 'Japanese'); the assertive or public phases inevitably invite comparisons with the original models, when the Japanese version usually appears to fail. (In passing, it is interesting to note that the Emperors and the aristocracy in general have consistently favoured indigenous and introspective tendencies in the arts.) For instance, Japanese examples of calligraphy in the regular Chinese script of *kaishu* or semi-cursive *xingshu* styles, by even the greatest monks who had lived and studied in China during the ninth and tenth centuries, cannot compare at first glance, in nobility, gravity or structual prowess, with corresponding examples by great Chinese masters. On the other hand, it is difficult for the non-Japanese to detect the 'japanization', the tendency towards a more sensuous line reflected in the Japanese hand. In Muromachi ink landscapes which reflect the Chinese Xia Gui style, connoisseurs of the Chinese prototypes lament the unhealthy appearance of the trees, the lack of solidity in the rocks and coherence in the pictorial structure, but do not see that in Japanese hands it is not the rocks and trees which represent early fifteenth-century ideals but the expansive, evocative space for which the trees and rocks serve merely as points of departure. In the same way, in the 'post-Impressionist' paintings of Sakamoto Hanjirō (1889–1956), it is not so much that his horses lack muscular structure or that his space lacks definition; what matters is the way in which his brush-strokes, oil-textures and choice of colours all help to convey a mood of autumnal gloom.

In the last twelve hundred years or so, when most imported cultural stimuli reached Japan from China, what was the response of the Japanese artist? How did he select and transform his models? These questions are some of the great fascinations of Japanese art, and the solutions found are an index to its supreme vitality and durability. For no two peoples could be more disparate. The ancestor-worshipping Chinese, for example, developed a sinewy, three-dimensional ideographic script for their monosyllabic language, and constructed a moral philosophy based on a profound respect for man and the brotherhood of all mankind. A great deal of Chinese imports to Japan thus reflect concern with continuation of lineages and permanence. The polysyllabic Japanese, on the other hand, communicates with whimsical deities through songs and dances, and his poetry is permitted the minutest emotive indulgences. With no eye on eternity, he quickens at the sight of unexpected beauty and cherishes its impermanence.

In the Heian period, aristocratic Japanese courtiers personally directed the development of indigenous art-forms and revealed their natural preference for the motifs (subdued colours, rolling contours, seasonal flowers) natural to the Yamato plains where they lived. Since these were totally unlike the 'monumental' vistas of granite peaks and vast distances characteristic of Chinese landscape-painting, the result was a transformation of Chinese source-material so profound that its Chinese origins

9

became irrelevant. (By contrast with this delicate art, intended for private enjoyment, public images in Heian halls of state, like the outsize murals of Chinese-style worthies ranged in strict vertical parallel, reflect the protective mirror of image-makers seeking parity with the outside world.)

In view of their relationship, it is worth discussing in general the differences between Chinese and Japanese art. Chinese forms tend to be self-contained and relaxed, while Japanese forms are affected by the overall composition of a picture, and emotional tension charges both motifs and the space around and between them. The inward-directed motifs of Chinese paintings tend to stress solidity and depth (an effect often achieved by the complex interweaving of brushstrokes), whereas the motifs in Japanese painting, each conceived as part of a larger emotional whole, tend to reach laterally across the picture-plane in a 'layered' technique, and to be drawn together by the treatment of the intervening space. The ease and grandeur of Chinese art generate forms which are malleable: each can be slightly changed in space without disturbing the overall visual harmony. Japanese art, by contrast, is often focussed on nuances of emotion, and works tend to be so charged with tension that altering the position of any part would drastically change the overall effect.

This intense feeling for texture, colour, form and space is intended to satisfy the spectator's need for emotional assurance and calm. Stepping-stones leading to a gate, for example, slow the visitor's pace. In a tea-

1 Stepping-stones laid in moss: a characteristic garden path.

2 *Bizen* unglazed vase showing straw marks, with asymmetrical ear-loop handles. Momoyama. (See p. 156)

3 *Kōgō*, incense-box, shaped like the comic character Oto Gozei. Earthenware, with overglaze enamels. Edo.

house interior, a feeling of calm is generated by the asymmetry of the space and the warm hues and 'woolly' textures of the surfaces. The Way of Tea in particular highlights this aspect of Japanese sensibility, where environment is structured to induce contemplation and calm, to promote a sense of social equality and brotherhood lacking in the rigid social hierarchies of the real world. Japanese critics express their preference for Korean peasant ware over the cool perfection of Chinese celadons by saying that 'the imperfect Korean bowl waits for me even when I am not at home, whereas the Chinese bowl waits for no one.' This statement reflects that perception of the inter-relationship of human beings and objects which permeates Japanese life, and which causes their 'worship of the imperfect' (i.e. the natural). A smooth celadon bowl, like the majestic Chinese landscape, is too perfect, too awesome: to the Japanese eye it seems severe, it 'waits for no one', and does not need human sympathy, 'audience participation', to visualize its innate perfection.

From the first moment we look at Japanese art, we are invited to relate in a personal way to the human qualities of imperfection built into the artwork, to the beauty of rooms with unadorned walls and textured surfaces, to artefacts like unglazed Bizen pottery, where straw wrappings 2 have been fired to leave uneven markings on the body; we are invited to discover the strong emotive qualities of an anonymous water-jar or dish, the wit of an incense-box shaped like an actress, or the deliberate 3 formality of a dinner-service created for a noble patron. In each case the artist gives himself wholly to the work, and reveals an unparalleled awareness of his medium, to the peculiarities of which he responds in a symbiotic way. There is no boundary between planes, between art and man.

Nothing expresses a people's spirit more than its folk crafts, and Japan's *mingei* have dazzled art-lovers around the world. Here generosity of spirit, love of simplicity, and perception of beauty in all natural things is
4 manifest. The simple Japanese farm-house, for example, with its rough-hewn wooden beams, unpainted walls and thatched roof, inspired the highly sophisticated, tea-house oriented *sukiya* architecture so influential
5 today. In simple lacquers such as the horned wine-bucket, exactly the same kind of peasant strength and forthrightness are expressed. There is no nervousness here about symmetry or glossy surfaces; indeed, there is a relaxed sophistication often lacking in the arts of the ruling classes.

In every facet of life, the Japanese have always devoted themselves to bringing about that sense of peace and harmony, of warmth and comfort, which they feel to be an essential part of beauty. In a Japanese meal, for example, quantities which would seem alarmingly frugal to a Chinese gourmet are attractively arranged in a variety of vessels, and are served in slow and graceful sequence on lacquered trays. Quantity is not a concern.

Instead, Japanese consciousness works through an aesthetic appreciation of the entire physical and psychological context of the meal. This includes seasonal as well as social considerations, but above all it satisfies the diner's senses. The timing of the dishes, and their appearance in bowls of varied shape, decoration and materials, are beautifully harmonized. The hungry Chinese would perhaps be astonished to realize that the feeling of satisfaction arises not from gorging oneself, but from savouring the carefully timed harmony of the food and its service (even down to matters like the waitresses' walk and gesture). Appreciation of such subtleties is essential to the enjoyment of Japanese culture in general, and of its arts in particular.

In the same way, the key to understanding the relationship of the Japanese artist or craftsman to his work lies in one word: union. Whether it be the chopstick-rest one finds in a fish restaurant, or a signed painting, one sees a particularly developed artistic sensibility at work. Painters of old caught exactly this quality of creative absorption in their depictions of carpenters, tatami floor-mat and bamboo-blind makers and mounters of paintings. In literature, the perfection of *renga* or linked verse is believed to come only through repeated group practice among the poets. More than in any other culture, Japanese poets incorporate each other's essence; potters incorporate the essence of the potting process (including finger-

4 *Minka*, farm-house, of the Tsubokawa family. Late 17th century.

5 Horned *sake* cask. Black lacquer. H. 57 cm. 19th century.

prints and kiln accidents); woodworkers or print-makers incorporate woodgrain and chisel marks as an integral and essential part of the finished work.

The artist and his materials, clay, wood or ink-brush and paper, together create the work. This factor is of paramount importance. Considerations basic to other cultures, such as personal uniqueness, the obliteration of all traces of the creative process (such as rough edges, fingerprints or chisel marks), as well as preconceived margins or the distinction of planes, are often of no importance. A six-sided Japanese box may be decorated in one continuous design which surrounds the form and unifies the planes. The common – and curious – practice in other cultures of decorating ceramic vessels in arbitrary horizontal strata is joyfully absent from Japanese ceramics, where decoration and form are aspects of a single whole.

When patrons demanded imported qualities unpalatable to Japanese taste (such as unequivocal statement, regularity, repetition, hard or shiny surfaces, equilateral symmetry, monumentality, rigid spaces in roads or rooms – in short, any qualities which stress self-sufficiency), the artist's response was usually to adjust and transform in accordance with his own feeling and personal taste. Philosophy, interest in building up in depth (whether in architectural space or dense brushstrokes on a painting surface), concepts of permanence and immutability are to a large extent alien. But these qualities are often precisely those which generated the Chinese forms which later entered Japan, and it is with this basic incompatibility in mind that we must watch Japan's genius unfold, untiringly transforming the continental model to suit its own expression. The poet Shinkei (1406–75) describes the way to artistic maturity thus (the italics are mine):

> Unless a verse is by one whose very being has been transfixed
> by the truth of the *impermanence* and *change* of this world,
> so that he is never forgetful of it in any circumstance,
> it cannot truly hold *deep feeling*.

CHAPTER TWO

Prehistoric Period (11th mil. BC–6th c. AD)

Japanese archaeology is the oldest and most systematic in East Asia. At its official centenary in 1977, 100,000 sites had been documented, yielding a fascinating array of artefacts ranging from Paleolithic tool-kits to Mesolithic and Neolithic ceramics. Many of these are so distinct in style from those of Japan's immediate continental neighbours as to suggest possible migrations from as far west as northern Europe.

Its geographical situation, at the eastern extreme of the Asian continental land mass, may have made prehistoric Japan the terminal point for numerous cultural migrations by peoples from Europe, Central Asia and the Altaic Mountain range, and Siberia. Seafaring peoples from South China, Southeast Asia and the Polynesian isles have also left their cultural imprint on Japanese architecture, regional dances and vowel structure.

From earliest times, the blend of differing cultural styles is evident. The ceramic strata unearthed by archaeology reveal legacies from cultures widely differing in social structure, religious ceremonies and cuisine.

Archaeologists divide the Japanese Paleolithic Age into two periods, Early (50,000–30,000 BC) and Late (30,000–11,000 BC). The division comes with technological evolution from crude and simple scrapers and cutting tools to more sophisticated blades, knives and small tools for engraving, drilling, scraping and piercing.

Jōmon culture (11,000–300 BC)

Japanese archaeologists date the following, or Mesolithic, period (characterized by a hunting, fishing and gathering way of life) from 11,000–300 BC. It is also called by the blanket name Jōmon ('cord-impressed'), after the distinctive surface decoration of its pottery. (However, the very first pottery of all (11,000–*c.* 7500) is startlingly different from what followed, and more closely resembles the work of Neolithic societies elsewhere in the world. These early vessels were quickly and easily made, by kneading and punching in the hand, and utilized the natural qualities of clay. They had smooth sides and generous interiors, enabling easy storage and retrieval, as befits utilitarian vessels used for food; they were sparingly decorated. Some scholars term this ware 'incipient-' or 'proto-' Jōmon, suggesting a continuity and internal development between it and Jōmon wares. But the new ware, 'Archaic' or 'Earliest' Jōmon, suggests markedly different attitudes to ceramic form and also to everyday eating and living. It seems doubtful that both styles could have come from a single developing culture; It would be more appropriate therefore to call this earliest phase pre-Jōmon.)

Archaic or Earliest Jōmon ware first appeared around 7500 BC. Examples have been found along the whole main archipelago from Hokkaidō to Okinawa, and on outlying islands such as Tsūshima, Sado, Oki and the Izu isles. It is highly textured, incised or cord-impressed, and has the qualities of low-relief sculpture. It is usually built up from piled or coiled clay rings, hand-joined inside and outside, and the outer surface is entirely covered with texture decoration, painstakingly applied. The typical pot is conical in form with a sharply pointed bottom, a flaring, often quatrifoil rim and a constricted and inaccessible interior. This form is far more difficult and time-consuming to make than are pots with open interiors such as the pre-Jōmon ware. Even more time-consuming is the application of the cord marks (by rolling a cord-covered stick smartly along the still damp, fragile surface of the clay cone), even if the pot were upturned with the point on top. For ordinary household storage or cooking, such elaborate effort far exceeds necessity and one must ask: what was the real function of these early vessels which were un-pot-like, hard to make, unlidded and impractical?

Middle Jōmon sees even more extraordinary developments. The base is flattened, the rim rises majestically to a height equalling the vessel body, and the lip is often topped with rippling scallops. The entire surface is alive with curvilinear, high-raised decoration with writhing coils forming spirals, S-shapes and meanders; the soaring, flame-like loops are charged with an intensity suggesting an outreach toward the supernatural. There is still a marked absence of 'tableware': bowls, dishes, cups, ewers or amphorae. Vessels of the period are mostly elaborate urns or jars, and were probably used for making ritual offerings.

In the Late Jōmon period (2500 BC onwards) another dramatic change reflects the arrival of a ceramic-rooted culture which emphasized the natural properties and forms of clay. There is a hint of Central Asian styles, with double-rhyton-shaped vessels, pouring vessels with open and closed spouts and short, squat, lidded pots with cylindrical spouts attached. Bowls and round-bottomed vessels reappear, as well as amphorae with narrowed necks and serving-bowls with handles. These

6 *Umataka* fired clay
urn in basketwork
form. H. 32 cm.
Middle Jōmon.

indicate a major shift in culinary habits, which includes the discovery of fermentation. (The new typological development, however, retains the raised surface designs characteristic of Jōmon ware.)

From 1000–300 BC (Terminal Jōmon), stemmed ware began to appear: shallow serving-bowls and amphorae with long narrow necks. These suggest acquaintance with wheel-thrown ware, though they themselves remain hand-built. Once again, the exact function of some vessels is hard to determine. A stemmed dish with an openwork dome, reminiscent of metalwork, for example, could have been used as an oil lamp or a hand-warmer.

It would seem that Jōmon culture did not develop entirely in isolation during its ten thousand year span, and that significant changes in Jōmon man's habits were periodically introduced. Aside from its spectacular pottery, Jōmon culture produced decorated blades of ivory, horn and bone, bracelets and earrings.

For his spiritual needs, Jōmon man carved figurines from stone and moulded them in clay. At about the same time that Middle Jōmon pottery urns were developing elaborate features, these figurines also underwent a dramatic transformation. Previous figurines had minimal facial features (such as a pinched nose and punctures for eyes); mid-Jōmon figurines have raised-line eyebrows and rather startling eyes: large perforations, round or almond shaped. By Late Jōmon (2500–1000 BC) they assume a

7 Clay figurine showing crown-shaped hair and 'insect' eyes. H. 31.7 cm. Terminal Jōmon.

8 (*opposite*) *Nonakado* stone group in 'sundial' arrangement at the centre of a burial pit. Late Jōmon.

mask-like quality and in some areas become highly ornate with shamanistic features surmounted by all kinds of decorative paraphernalia. At the end of the period, in Terminal Jōmon (1000–300 BC), extremely
7 sophisticated vessels and figures appear. The hollow body (whether of pot or figurine) is covered with elaborate, raised cord-impressed patterns and the figurines have enormous insect or shell shaped eyes. This kind of cord-impressed pattern, over a plain 'cord-erased' background, is a particularly sophisticated use of 'negative' (ie, undecorated) space. (Although their ritual use is still unknown, these late figurines have such enormous, horizontally slitted eyes that some scholars say they are the product of an age of deep superstition and fear; it is, however, difficult to reconcile superstition and fear with the uninhibited decoration also characteristic of these artefacts, which seems far more readily attributable to Jōmon man's exuberance and general delight in 'the dance of life'.)

The most significant religious legacy of the Jōmon period is the stone
8 circles and menhirs found in the Tōhoku area in Akita and further north in Hokkaidō, some measuring as much as thirty metres across. Each centres on a square burial-pit in which bones were placed, covered with pebbles.

18

These tombs resemble those found in Siberia from the Bronze Age into the early Iron Age. A peculiarly Japanese feature of each site, however, is the placing of a large upright stone in the centre from which other long stones, laid flat, radiate like the spokes of a wheel. This sundial-like arrangement suggests an agrarian society, aware of seasonal changes; but the link – if any – with the following Yayoi culture is not yet clear.

Yayoi culture (c. 300 BC–c. AD 300)

Yayoi culture derives its name from the characteristic wheel-thrown pottery first discovered at the Yayoi site near Tokyo. This is entirely different from Jōmon ware. Some scholars believe that the Yayoi (called the Wa or Wo people by Chinese chroniclers) were the first people to settle in Japan whom we might recognize as Japanese today. They arrived from the continent and settled on the southern tip of the Korean peninsula and in northern Kyūshū. They had a highly civilized technology of bronze and iron, wheel-thrown ceramics and wet-rice cultivation. Their sea-borne trade flourished, reaching as far as Lolan, the Han Commandery in Northern Korea. They drove the Jōmon people north and south; though traces of Jōmon styles of pot-decoration remained in northern Japan throughout the Yayoi period, elsewhere (beginning in northern

Kyūshū and spreading gradually through Honshū) wheel-thrown Yayoi pottery effectively replaced the earlier Jōmon ware.

Ceramics of the Yayoi period included combed bowls, jars with wide bellies and flaring necks, lidded jars and tall urns. Towards the middle Yayoi period there began to appear goblets, narrow-necked bottles, high-footed wide dishes, ewers and handled cups. All of these indicate a high level of skill with the potter's wheel: it is clear that 'tableware' had now begun to replace purely functional or ritual pots. (The existence of vessels containing traces of grain confirms the agrarian nature of this age.)

The new, wheel-thrown wares have smooth surfaces, and the red or incised decoration tends to be horizontal, combed or zigzag bands across the vessel. This contrasts with the tactile surface and predominantly vertical decoration of Jōmon pottery.

Since metallurgy was introduced to Japan and not indigenously developed, bronze and iron appeared simultaneously around the third century BC. But the introduced forms were quickly adapted to serve the needs of Yayoi man: bronze war-swords from the continent, for example, became, in the hands of native craftsmen, broader and longer peace-swords for use in burials. One of the most striking importations of all was the *dōtaku* bronze bell, with its characteristic oval shape and protruding flanges. At first these bells were small, but they were gradually made larger and larger, and were often adorned in twelve sections to symbolize the twelve-month year. The magical *ryūsui*, or flowing-water designs (C- or S-spirals in bands of parallel raised lines) meander in zigzags. (These patterns are also found on pottery and tombs; they became part of the later Japanese artistic vocabulary.) Some of the later bells rise splendidly in majesty, with double C-spirals extending beyond the flanges which are now entirely ornamental; they may have been used in ritual, perhaps as symbols of state. *Dōtaku* bells are found in isolated areas, far from settlements and carefully buried. They seem a purely Yayoi phenomenon; certainly they were never made again once the Kofun culture appeared.

While intimate Yayoi contact with Korea is well documented, evidence also suggests some form of direct contact with China. A great number of Chinese bronzes, especially Han mirrors, have been found in Yayoi sites, far more numerous than those found in Korea and those of Korean manufacture. This suggests not only direct contact with China, but also a marked selectivity on the part of the Yayoi when it came to imported artefacts.

Mirrors, *dōtaku*, ceremonial swords, and cashew-nut-shaped jades and agates (*magatama* or Korean fertility jewels) are the principal ritual art objects of the Yayoi period. They are propitiatory objects, and show

9 Clay pitcher showing horizontal decoration and openwork footrim. H. 22 cm.
Mid-Yayoi.

10 *Dōtaku* ritual bronze bell. H. 44.8 cm. Late Yayoi. (Note the similar shape of the
Kofun tomb below.)

11 Aerial view of the thrice-moated 'keyhole' tumulus of Emperor Nintoku.
Kofun.

dependence on the land and the weather. The robust, surface-oriented sculptural forms of the Jōmon hunter give way to more stately, noble vessels more demonstrative of the potter's craft: exterior shape conforms to interior space, and the decoration is simple and understated. Quiet dignity is achieved through purified forms.

Compared to the previous Jōmon or subsequent Kofun cultures, the Yayoi seem to have been particularly civilized, peaceful and refined, using advanced technology to bring about a rise in living standards and to contribute to a religious consciousness which seems more rational and serene than in other periods. It is in the time of the Yayoi that a preference for artistic purity, in both form and decoration, first appears. This purity is the quintessential expression of Shintō (Way of the Gods), the spiritual belief and practice which is thought to have developed about this time. The *kami* or super-consciousness is thought to reside everywhere: in ancient trees, in enormous boulders, in elevated wooden shrines plainly made and without decoration. The love of unadorned materials and pristine freshness, those fundamental attributes of Japanese art, first found expression in the Yayoi period.

The Kofun period (300–600 AD)

The third and last prehistoric period is named after its characteristic tumuli, or *Kofun*: huge, mounded tombs, at first round, then keyhole-shaped.

The earlier tombs, found in many areas, from southern Kyūshū to northern Tōhoku, number in the thousands. The earliest of all are concentrated in the Yamato Plains, and continue the traditions of Yayoi culture. (It may even be argued that the early Kofun tombs are actually an extension of Yayoi burial practice. The use of cosmic mirrors, for example, is common to both.) The grandest tombs of all are close in time and are not found inland, but on the Kawachi Plain in Osaka Prefecture, near the Inland Sea. They are Imperial mausolea, and the finest of them, such as those of the Emperors Ōjin (reigned *c.* 346–95) and Nintoku (reigned *c.* 395–427) are situated by the port, suggesting that these early rulers had come into Japan from the continent, via northern Kyūshū, advancing along the Inland Sea to the Kinai region, where they settled.

11   The largest mausoleum is that of the Emperor Nintoku. It consists of a rounded, keyhole-shaped mound with trapezoidal elevations in front (thought to have been a ritual altar). If we include the three surrounding moats, the total length of the tomb is 480 metres, and at its highest point the mound rises to 35 metres. The area is 110,950 square metres (about

458 acres); the total volume 1,405, 866 cubic metres. The archaeologist Umehara Sueji has calculated that if one person could move about one cubic metre of earth a day, it would have taken 1000 people, working daily, four years to complete the mound.

A characteristic feature of Kofun tombs is pottery figures called *haniwa*. These first appeared (as jars with stands) in the Okayama region facing the Inland Sea; later (in the fourth century) they became cylindrical and were placed 'on guard' around the central area of each tomb; later still they were placed in concentric circles enclosing an earthen platform at whose centre was the pottery house, thought to be the abode of the dead person's soul, and also surrounded by pottery shields and ceremonial sunshades. At the end of the fourth century, *haniwa* became anthropomorphic, hollow figures dressed in minutely detailed costumes. During the sixth century animals (chickens, horses, wild boar, deer, dogs, cats, cattle and fish) were added. These were placed in rows facing outwards, above ground; the sacred central area was reserved for birds, boats and houses,

12 *Haniwa* figure: farmer carrying plough blade. H. 92 cm. Excavated from a tomb. Late Kofun.

presumably linked symbolically with the transport of the soul to its final resting-place.

12   The human *haniwa* figures – many with deep-set eyes and abundant curly hair, suggesting a race distinctly non-Japanese – give a fascinating glimpse of the society which created them. They include falconers, grooms, farmers, soldiers in armour, priestesses, ladies of the court, and musicians and dancers posed as if performing for the deceased.

From the fifth century onwards, Kofun artefacts begin to suggest the presence of a new, equestrian and military culture. (It is as yet un-named, and has no specific terminal dates; but the evidence of the artwork suggests that it was authoritarian and martial, distinctly at variance with the agrarian and peaceable society of Yayoi and early Kofun.) It shares features with the contemporary Silla culture of Southern Korea, and many types of artefacts appear on both sides of the Tsushima Straits. There are gilt-bronze accoutrements of the mounted archer: crowns adorned with 'branches' from which hang golden leaves and *magatama* jewels, bronze stirrups, openwork pommels and peaked golden helmets; even domestic objects like mirrors and bracelets are often adorned with horsebells. A bronze crown is surmounted by horses in silhouette, and by jingling leaf-discs. Finally there is the Silla/Sueki ware, a thin, high-fired, dark pottery in metallic forms with jingling attachments. (There are stylistic affinities here with Scythian and Central Asian cultures: not only the tree-imagery and the openwork design, but motifs like the gryphon and palmette, imported from even further west. The enormous range of trade as far as the Middle East is shown by the presence, in one sixth-century tomb, of a glass bowl made in Persia.)

13   A striking late Kofun development in Kyūshū was the dolmen type of tomb, whose stone-lined inner chambers had decorated walls and sometimes contained stone sarcophagi decorated with incised or painted designs. (The colours are red hematite, black charcoal, yellow ochre, white china clay and green chlorite.) The earliest of these tombs (those in the centre of present-day Kumamoto) are decorated with red and black diamond patchwork. Later, painted tombs appeared over a wider area; those in the northern area of Fukuoka are decorated with the figures of horses, grooms, birds and boats as well as with the magic spirals and concentric circles found elsewhere. Large drawings of quivers, and double C-coils, are prominent, as are the horses, birds and boats associated with the soul's last journey.

The most striking image which can be associated with the Kofun period is the decorative motif known as the *chokkomon* ('straight-lines-and-arcs'). This consists of a series of broken arcs drawn over opposed diagonals or

13 Takehara dolmen wall painting of man leading a horse. Late Kofun.

14 Bronze mirror showing *chokkomon* design. 5th century.

crosses, and was apparently made using compasses and a ruler. The *chokkomon* design is found in places and on objects associated with burial: incised, for example, on the walls of tombs and sarcophagi, or part of the decoration of *haniwa* quivers and bronze mirrors. It is one of the first of those striking conjunctions of straight and curved lines which became such a prominent feature of later Japanese art.

14

CHAPTER THREE

Asuka and Nara (552–794)

Shintō shrines

The religious practice of the early Japanese was based on a profound sense of awe for natural manifestations such as sun, water, trees, rocks, sound and silence. Man's response to these phenomena was to purify himself and to identify sacred precincts. Much later this practice was named Shintō (Way of the Gods), to distinguish it from Buddhism which had entered Japan in the sixth century, bringing with it a full panoply of architecture, doctrine and indoor ceremonies. Although later Shintō developed its own architecture, art, clergy and forms of ritual, it is essentially an indigenous religion with neither dogma, scriptures nor form.

It seems safe to say that the earliest sacred precincts were places of particular beauty, demarcated by rudimentary stone boundaries and by simple, pre-architectural monuments (such as rock piles surmounted by stones) indicating the places where sacred presences were first sensed. Monuments of this kind still survive in the precincts of the Ise Jingū. Here worship took its purest form, in total silence with no ritual. (Construction of the earliest Shintō shrines seems related to palace architecture of the Tumulus period, and is characterized by simplicity of both form and material.) In the Ise Jingū precinct, a raised-floor building with a giant thatched gable supported by nine huge pillars is reached by an outside ladder, set at a steep angle. (Reconstructions of another ancient site, Izumo Taisha, in western Japan, facing Korea, suggest a particular sense 15 of mystery and also the intimacy, darkness and warmth associated with the sacred domain of the spirit or *kami*. The worshipper climbs a long flight of steps and, once inside the hall, proceeds beyond the central pillar and turns right to the innermost quadrant before reaching the *sanctum sanctorum*. All this is in marked contrast to the foursquare centrality of Buddhist architecture, where icon images dominated huge open spaces in stone-paved, ground level monastic halls.)

The Ise Jingū, on the eastern coast, is both the ancestral shrine of the 16 imperial family and the national shrine. It has been rebuilt every twenty years since the reign of Emperor Temmu (reigned 672–686), fifty-nine

15 Izumo Taisha Shintō shrine (rebuilt 1744), showing covered stairway (and Main Sanctuary with deep thatch).

16 (*opposite*) Aerial view of Ise Jingū showing Naikū's two sectors. Site dates from the 4th century.

times altogether by 1973. The space is dominated by two compounds, the western Naikū and the eastern Gekū, thought to have been first built in the fourth and late fifth centuries respectively. They are dedicated to Amaterasu Ōmikami (Heaven-illuminating Great Spirit, the daughter of Izanagi no Mikoto), traditional ancestor of the imperial house, and to Toyoukeno Ōkami (Great Spirit of Food Abundance and grandson of Izanagi no Mikoto, provider of the Five Grains). The site is among tall evergreens near the Isuzu River; its cool stillness is broken only by the clatter of cleanwashed pebbles underfoot, and it is said to have been chosen by Amaterasu herself, in an apparition to Princess Yamato early in the first century AD.

Each compound is divided into an eastern and western sector; when one sector is in use, the other is kept empty, white and still, with its ground-covering of pebbles. Each compound is rectilinear, enclosed by four layered wooden fences. The buildings are aligned along the central north-south axis, beginning with thatched and gabled gates set into the southern fences. The main sanctuary (or *shōden*), three bays wide and two bays deep, is poised aloft on a structure of pillars and surrounded by a covered veranda. The approach is by a stairway leading to the central bay. Some elements, such as alignment, the layered enclosure and the metal decorative accents may be later features incorporated from continental architecture, but distinguishing native characteristics remain: the roof with its forked finials pointing skywards at either end, the heavy ridge course topped by cylindrical, tapered billets laid crosswise along the ridge, and the main pillars which are embedded directly in the ground, not set in foundations. The general impression is of abstract design, of planes, angles, circles in simple but dynamic interaction. The natural colours and textures of the wood and pebbles are not sullied; the effect is warm; the atmosphere is one of intimacy and awe.

In spite of the arrival and dominance of Buddhism, Shintō shrines continued to be built in serene woods and beside quiet shores, and were later often incorporated into Buddhist compounds, representing as they did local manifestations of universal Buddhist values. Shintō silence, its simplicity and its direct yet undefined interaction between man and nature or spirits are characteristic Japanese additions to, or modifications of, imported religion, just as the same qualities modify imported art.

The introduction of Buddhism, striking as it did at the core of Japanese spiritual consciousness, exerted a profound and far-reaching effect upon all aspects of Japanese life. The higher presence (or *kami*), of which the Japanese were so intensely aware, and which possessed no specified form or attribute, now appeared in a plethora of human guises. Principles of the faith were expounded in Chinese texts and by the clergy; regiments of monks and nuns performed minutely prescribed religious functions inside vast halls filled with anthropomorphic statues, illumined with candles and befogged with incense. The stillness was broken by chanting to the beat of drums, gongs and bells.

With the coming of Buddhism, Japan was introduced to a concept of systems, routines and regulations. Buddhism channelled silent and spontaneous interaction with spirits into an organized programme of ritual observance, and explained the mysteries of life by the Law of Cause and Effect. The new theology, with its inexorable focus on the after-life, must have both disturbed and inspired followers of Shintō, who suddenly found previously vague sentiments now clearly articulated and vigorously systematized. The Aryan mind of India had been absorbed in metaphysical subtleties for centuries and had learned to analyse phenomena and control consciousness even before the birth of Gautama (567–488 BC), the historical Buddha. After attaining total enlightenment the Buddha explained that existence is a continuing series of transformations and that salvation from suffering and death lies in detachment from desires.

Buddhism arrived in Japan from Korea after centuries of development in China. The king of Paekche (Kudara) in the south-eastern corner of the Korean peninsula presented a gilt-bronze image of Buddha to Emperor Kimmei of Japan in 552 AD, with the assurance that 'this doctrine can create religious merit and retribution without measure or bounds, and lead one to a full appreciation of the highest wisdom'. The emperor, who had no wish to offend native spirits, was grateful but cautious: he allowed the powerful Soga family to practise the new religion before all others.

In fact, many members of the immigrant community in Japan had practised Buddhism for years prior to 552. The Korean scholar Wani is recorded to have introduced (Chinese) writing to Japan in 405; other immigrants, in charge of various *be* (hereditary guilds specializing in painting, weaving, saddlery) had settled in the Yamato area during the reign of Emperor Yūryaku (457–79). During the Asuka period, every major building project used imported Korean specialists, many of whom subsequently settled. (Although immigrant Chinese craftsmen are mentioned, some families for several generations, artistic contact, like religious contact, between Japan and China, was largely by way of Korea. Korean dress was worn at court, as evidenced by the two Paradise embroidery panels (*Tenjūkoku Mandala*) produced by court ladies for the repose of Prince Shōtoku's soul in 623: see page 35.)

Prince Shōtoku (573–621) and the rise of Buddhism

The Asuka period is particularly notable for the life and activities of Prince Umayado, better known by his Buddhist name Shōtoku (Sagely and Virtuous), an avid scholar and learned statesman whose cultural activities substantially advanced Japanese civilization at this time. In the arts, the period reflects cultural links with the Korean peninsula rather than with China, in particular with the kingdoms of Koguryō to the north and Paekche to the southwest.

Born into a court which had been receiving Buddhist images from Korea for twenty-one years and which was coming to terms with the new faith, Shōtoku grew up in an atmosphere of cultural ferment. The powerful pro-Buddhist Soga clan was withstanding pressure from conservative elements (notably from the custodian of Shintō rituals, Nakatomi, and the military chief Mononobe, who together burned down chapels built on Soga instructions, and hurled their Buddhist statues into the Naniwa canal). Soga no Umako (died 626) placed his niece on the throne as Empress Suiko (reigned 592–628) and ordered Prince Shōtoku, then only nineteen years old, to act as Regent. This turned out to be Soga's greatest deed, and the Suiko reign saw the rise of a literate culture that permeated the social and political life of the aristocracy.

Prince Shōtoku was an ardent Buddhist scholar. At court he lectured and wrote commentaries on the Vimalakirti sūtra, the *shōman-gyō*, and the Lotus sūtra. In 607 he dispatched a scholar to Sui China to study Buddhism and ordered the first compilation of the history of Japan (now lost). In 604 he had decreed the famous Seventeen Articles, aiming at social harmony, in an attempt to centralize power and to unify the various clan-chiefs whose rivalries had hitherto dominated Japanese life.

The Prince built his palace at Ikaruga overlooking the Yamato River (which flowed to nearby Naniwa, gateway to Korea). Next to it he built a Buddhist temple, called the Wakakusadera. Soga no Umako built another temple, the Hōkōji, in 596. (Both this and the Wakakusadera were laid out in imitation of contemporary Paekche style, with the southern gate close to the inner gate, and the sūtra repository, belfry and lecture hall to the north, outside the compound.) By 614, over half a century since the

17 Aerial view of Hōryūji compound, pagoda to west, Golden Hall to east. Late 7th century.

presentation of the first Buddhist statue to Japan, there were 46 temples and 1385 ordained monks and nuns.

After Shōtoku's death the Soga clan sought to replace his influence with their own, arrested his son, and killed or forced his family to suicide. They burnt down the Ikaruga Palace in 643, and in 670 burnt the Wakakusadera itself. However, Shōtoku's legacy, the primacy of learning and of moral values, had been so firmly implanted among the aristocracy and the clergy that the ruined temple was soon rebuilt. The new compound, now called the Hōryūji, lay to the northwest of the Wakakusadera site. The layout of the main original (continental) model (a rectilinear walled compound whose three basic structures – the *chūmon* or inner gate, the pagoda and the main, Golden Hall – were all aligned on a south-north axis, facing south) involved the worshipper in a progression from one holy building to another, in a straight line. The rebuilt compound, however, had its long side on the east-west axis, and the *chūmon* at the southern end, slightly to the west. The pagoda was now to the west, and the Golden Hall to the east; both were equidistant from the

32

chūmon and simultaneously visible to the worshipper as he entered. Instead of proceeding into the depths of the compound through a succession of buildings, the pilgrim now made a lateral turn. This eschewing of linear penetration in favour of lateral movement is one of the basic traits of japanization and is repeatedly met throughout Japanese history.

The Tamamushi Shrine

This portable shrine is the oldest architectural example surviving from the Asuka period. Housed in a temple which escaped burning, it was later moved to the Hōryūji. The bronze filigree bands ornamenting the pedestal and architectural members were once inlaid with the iridescent wings of the *tamamushi* beetle, hence its name. (Although the same type of beetle is found in Korea, the choice of camphor and cypress wood native to Japan is evidence of Japanese manufacture, some time during the late Asuka period (*c*. 650), when many of the statues for the original Wakakusadera were being produced.) The shrine's hipped and gabled roof is tiled in such a way as to mark a distinct break between the upper and lower portions, whereas the rebuilt Hōryūji temple has roofs tiled in one continuous plane, although the rafters beneath show a separation between the sharply pitched upper section and the more gently curving lower section. This method gives the roof an effect of curvature and lightness which is characteristic of Asuka architecture.

19

Asuka painting

Widescale destruction has left very little evidence of Asuka painting, but surviving works in lacquer and in embroidery hint at a thriving co-existence of styles imported from a variety of sources. On the Tamamushi shrine, for example, the lacquered wood is painted over with an oil-based paint in four colours. This *mitsuda-e* technique has distant origins in Persia and its appearance here has puzzled those who hold China's silk routes to be the only trading link between the Mediterranean and the Pacific. However, centuries of Scytho-Siberian activities in Korea are confirmed by the equestrian artefacts in metal found in royal tombs in Silla's Kyongjū area, almost identical to those excavated in Japan from the Kofun and the Asuka periods. Sillan golden drinking vessels pre-date those (admittedly more advanced) of mid-Tang China by nearly three centuries, and it is possible that Persian techniques were transmitted to Japan before China. It is reasonable to postulate a 'northern route' which

18, 19 Tiger *jātaka* (*left*), oil on lacquered cypress, the left panel from the base of the Tamamushi Shrine, and the Shrine itself (*right*), with its roof of camphor and cypress wood. Mid-7th century.

linked West to East, bypassing China. The actual style of the Tamamushi oil paintings, however, also transmitted through Korea, distinctly recalls Northern and Western Wei prototypes from China.

On the left panel of the base of the Tamamushi Shrine is a very early example of that style of narrative painting which achieved unparalleled heights in later Japanese art. It is a *jātaka* (a tale depicting one of the Buddha's previous lives). As Prince Mahāsattva hunts in the mountains with his two brothers, he comes upon a starving tigress and her seven cubs. The brothers flee, but Mahāsattva offers his own flesh for

18

nourishment. This act of compassion ensures advancement to Buddha-hood in a future life. The panel tells the story in three sequential scenes: on the cliff the prince doffs his robe; he plunges down the chasm; he is then shown at the bottom, being devoured by the grateful tigress. His body is lithe and graceful; the flowing lines and the tendency toward attenuation are characteristic of mid-century sculpture. The rock forms, also to be found in early Korean art, are derived from Six Dynasties painting. In mid-seventh century Japan we are already seeing sympathetic and sensitive reception of cultural and technical ideas from earlier Buddhist art. Its swift assimilation shows the enormous appeal of the new religion.

When Shōtoku Taishi died, a pair of paradise tapestries (*Tenjūkoku Mandala*) was ordered in 622, to be handsewn by court ladies. The designers were immigrant artists from Korea and China. Surviving fragments show figures in contemporary Koguryō dress. It is highly 20 probable that the prince and his court wore Koguryō style robes in life. The Sui-Tang style robe in which he is shown in the famous posthumous painting of which a copy survives, now in the Imperial Collection, is doubtless a fabrication of Nara artists in the flush of Chinese fashions and an anachronism. Korean elements permeated the lifestyles of the aristo-cracy throughout the seventh century. An eighth-century burial mound recently excavated at Takamatsu revealed murals of figures in Koguryō dress (now up-dated, reflecting Tang proportions and poses). It would seem that intimate relations with Korean royal households continued in

20 Tenjūkoku Mandala (detail). Embroidered silk. 622.

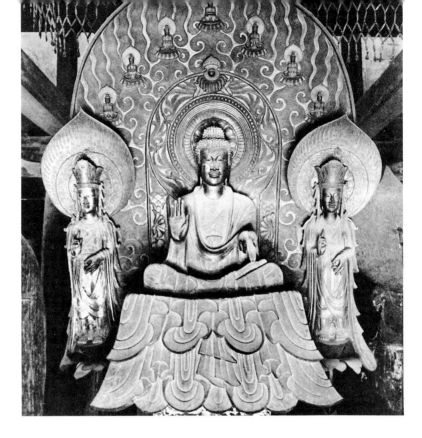

spite of the Chinese Sui and later Tang contacts, and that the transition from Korea-oriented to China-oriented styles was a gradual process.

Asuka sculpture

Shōtoku's principal Buddhist master was Hye-cha, a Koguryō monk whose state-oriented Buddhism (typical of Northern Wei China) differed from the politically more liberal southern Buddhism of Paekche and Liang China, where monks did not have to reverence the sovereign. However, the influence of Buddhist diplomats, monks, artisans and painters from both Korean kingdoms had been felt since the mid-sixth century. It can be assumed that a variety of contrasting styles flourished during the Suiko period; the Hōryūji temple alone reveals several artistic sources.

One source is non-Chinese, the Scytho-Siberian equestrian culture of the earlier Kofun period. This is seen both in the openwork metal crowns

21 Shaka Triad. Bronze.
Middle figure h. 86.3 cm,
attendants 91 cm. Hōryūji
Golden Hall, 623.

22 Guze Kannon (detail).
Gilded camphor wood. H.
197 cm. Early 7th century.

which Shiba Tori (significantly, a third-generation Chinese member of
the saddler's guild) used on his Buddhist sculptures (see below), and in the
panels of circles and triangles facing the overhead canopies (which recall
Kofun murals in the stone dolmens of Fukuoka and Kumamoto).

Another source is revealed in the angular, severe and archaistic
sculptural style of Shiba Tori's actual sculptures. Tori school works were
the official style of the Suiko reign; they include the Asuka Great Buddha
(cast for the Hōkōji temple in 606 and since extensively restored and
remodelled), the tall wooden standing statue of Guze Kannon made for
Prince Shōtoku before his death, the Yakushi Healing Buddha of 607,   22
whose gentleness presages that of the attendants in the Shaka Triad of 623,
and several of the so-called 'Forty-Eight (bronze) Statues of Hōryūji' now   21
in the Tokyo National Museum. These Tori works derive their regal
stiffness from sixth-century Koguryō bronze statuettes: they are conceived frontally, in terms of planes and tubes, and have typical facial
characteristics: the Buddha's eyes slant upwards, the nose is long, flared at

the bottom, and forms a conspicuous triangle in the ovoid, tube-like face, and the mouth is set close under the nose, which makes the chin appear large. The deep trough beneath the nose cuts into the upper lip, forming the Tori hall-mark: twin points rising at a prominent angle. The lips, in simple angled planes, are pulled back in the 'archaic smile', and the dimple beneath the lower lip is deeply etched. The neck is a smaller cylinder beneath that of the head; the shoulders are set four-square. The body is conceived as front-facing, upright blocks; the muscles lack articulation beneath the drapery. These characteristics link the Tori style, by way of Kogyurō reinterpretation, to earlier Chinese Wei sources.

Koguryō Buddhist philosophy may account for the stern mien of Tori's main figures, but mention should be made of the gently rounded and tender quality of his peripheral figures (for example the small seated Buddhas of the mandorla cast in relief), qualities common in the second half of the seventh century, but already evident in Tori's time. The meditating bodhisattva Maitreya in the Kōryūji is carved from a hollowed block of red pine, a tree which grows abundantly in Korea but not in Japan. (Japanese wooden sculptures are made either from camphor or Japanese cypress.) Its style and details are related to the famous gilt-bronze meditating bodhisattva in Seoul's Toksu Palace Museum. The eyebrows arch out and up; the eyes are narrow slits with a straight upper lid and the lower curved; the nose is narrow, and distinctly ridged. The groove beneath it flares as it reaches the lips which (unlike the simple lateral planes of the Tori school) bifurcate to left and right. The chin is less prominent than those in the Tori style, and the face more rounded. The body inclines gently forward, and the bare torso tapers inwards below the breast. An impression of gentleness and absorption is part of the sculptor's intention.

An exquisite bodhisattva in the Chūgūji convent in Hōryūji shares the characteristics of the Kōryūji figure and of the Toksu (Seoul) bodhisattva except that the downward-arching eyebrows here add an impression of maternal tenderness. (There are several sculptural affinities amongst the three pieces: the spherical modelling of the eyeballs, the articulation and inclination of the torsos, the proportion of arms and legs.) Unfortunately, we know nothing of the carving and dedication of this beautiful statue, but as it is housed in Hōryūji it may have been associated with Prince Shōtoku and Korea.

Recent investigations have established a Paekche provenance for the Toksu Palace Museum bodhisattva. In 541, King Songmyong of Paekche had sent to the Chinese Liang court for Buddhist texts, craftsmen and painters. The resultant softening of Paekche style in the latter sixth century can be seen not only in the Toksu gilt bronze meditating

23 Meditating Miroku Bosatsu (detail). Red Pine. Kōryūji, Kyoto. H. 123.5 cm. 603?

24 Meditating bodhisattva (detail). Camphor wood. Chūgūji convent. H. 87.5 cm. Early 7th century.

bodhisattva but also in its Kōryūji and Hōryūji sisters. In 603 Paekche presented a gilt seated meditating bodhisattva to Prince Shōtoku. The Prince charged a nobleman to worship it, and the nobleman built the Hachioka-dera (Kōryūji) to house it. From separate historical accounts scholars have identified the Kōryūji red pine Maitreya as the 603 Paekche statue. (Originally this work had been gilt.) The Chūgūji bodhisattva is made of the camphor wood typical of Japanese sculpture. Its remarkable resemblance to the Kōryūji and Toksu works, and the absence of its followers in Japan, suggest its being the work of a Korean sculptor, working perhaps in Japan. The presence of the soft contemporary Paekche style in Japan by the first decade of the seventh century may account for the softened contours of peripheral Tori school works even during this most severe and archaistic phase of Buddhist sculpture.

Another craftsman who, like Tori, was of Chinese descent and who worked in the Koguryō-derived angular style in Hōryūji, was Aya no Yamakuchi no Ōkuchi Atahi. Among other works, he produced the Four

25 Celestial Guardians or Heavenly Kings (*shitennō*) for the Golden Hall, some time before the Taika Reform of 646 (which ended the Soga clan's power and patronage). The Four Kings show an advance in volumetric and three-dimensional sculpture, even though they have the unmistakable archaistic Tori stamp. They are more rounded and the faces are fuller and more expressive. Many of the so-called 'Forty-Eight Buddhist Statues' originally associated with Hōryūji (now in the Tokyo National Museum) are of obvious Korean manufacture, but there are also several examples in the Tori style. In short, although during the pre-Taika period under Soga influence the severe northern Korean style was dominant, it coexisted with styles of southern Korean origin. After the Taika Reformation, however, gentler styles superseded the Tori style. Among the Forty-Eight Statues there are many with child-like proportions: large heads, hands and feet, and small bodies. The faces have highly arched, rounded eyebrows set high above heavy-lidded, narrow-slitted eyes; the noses are shorter than those of the Tori school, and the mouths are set lower, giving smaller, rounded and fleshy chins. This child-like style seems to have influenced many larger figures during the second half of the seventh century, the Hakuhō period, 645–710. For example, in the Kannon

26 figures of Kinryūji and Hōryūji (the hair parted in the middle, high above the brow and temple and looped over long ears), the beatific smile suggests innocence and the inner peace of meditation. The same child-like style appears in the flying wooden apsaras which adorn the canopy over the main figures in the Hōryūji's Golden Hall. Seated on lotus blossoms, and playing musical instruments, they appear to descend from heaven on flying tendrils. Although made during the Hakuhō period, such child-like works probably derive from the Paekche style seen in the tiny gilt-bronze Asuka figurines. True Hakuhō sculpture does not appear until the end of the seventh century, in the Yakushiji Triad.

The Hakuhō (White Phoenix) period 645–710

In the 660s, at the same time that Silla was conquering both Paekche and Koguryō, Chinese Tang was entering its most glorious phase. In Japan, as a result of the Taika reform and the removal of the Soga clan from power and patronage, the flood-gates were opened to Chinese influences. Hakuhō Japanese sculpture shows these influences in substantial works of imperial grandeur. There is new-found authority and grace; sculpture is rounded and more realistic.

One of the most powerful Hakuhō sculptures is the larger-than-life group of gilt-bronze statues in the Yakushiji. The seated Yakushi

25 (*left*) Zōchō Ten (Virudhaka), one of the four Guardian Kings from the Hōryūji. Carved wood. H. 20.7 cm. Before 646.

26 (*above*) One of six standing bodhisattvas (detail). Camphor wood. Style probably derived from Paekche. H. 85.7 cm. Late 7th century.

27 Gakkō, from Yakushi Triad. Gilt bronze. H. 315.3 cm. Hakuhō, 688.

28 Amida Triad, seated on lotus blooms, in Lady Tachibana's Shrine. Gilt bronze. H. 33 cm. 733.

29 Yumetagai Kannon. Bronze. H. 85.7 cm. Late Hakuhō.

27 (Healing Buddha) is flanked by two bodhisattvas, Nikkō (Sunlight) and Gakkō (Moonlight), for which there are no prototypes in the Hōryūji Treasure Museum or among the Forty-Eight statuettes. They are realistically conceived in the round rather than frontally, and are in *contraposto* stance, the weight on the inner foot, swinging the upper torso outwards. The faces are full, almost spherical and the chins droop toward the necks and thence to the chests, in three fleshy wrinkles. These bodhisattvas, like the Shō Kannon housed in the Kondō of the same temple, have upswept hair which culminates in a high topknot and is secured on the forehead with a trifoliate crown. Both the Shō Kannon and the Yakushi, perhaps because they are principal rather than flanking figures, are more conservative in style and have little turning of the torso, as the body weight is centred. These figures show a clear High Tang influence in their rounded lips and faces, and in their expressions of deep absorption. This influence may also be seen in the Hōryūji paradise murals.

Bronze sculpture in Hōryūji was more conservative in idiom and, even toward the end of the century, retained vestiges of the Tori style. Among

the most beautiful works here are the Yumetagai (Dream-changing) 29
Kannon and the Amida Triad of Lady Tachibana's Shrine. They have the 28
fuller proportions, characteristic chins and sloping necks of the Yakushiji
figures; but the facial modelling is rather restrained, with angular lines
along the brows, nose and lips (which rise in twin points and bear the Tori
cylindrical dimple beneath). More than any other works of the time, such
pieces seem to exude a full, aristocratic confidence, and may be the work
of conservative craftsmen who maintained Hōryūji traditions in the face
of imported Chinese styles and techniques. New artisans, however,
painted the Hōryūji murals and sculpted the extensive clay panorama of
Buddha's nirvana in the Hōryūji Pagoda.

These clay sculptures are built into niches in the four corners of the
pagoda and were completed in 711, one year after the capital moved to
Nara, the start of the Tempyō period. In a scene depicting the
conversation between the Buddhist layman and scholar Yuima (Vim-
alakīrti) and the bodhisattva Monjū (Mañjuśrī) the latter even looks as if 30
he could have stepped out of one of the newly-completed murals in the
Kondō (Golden Hall). Wearing flowing robes and a jewelled necklace, the

43

bodhisattva sits full-faced in regal pose, his wavy, backswept hair in a high topknot. The dress of the lay onlooker is in High Tang style. The concept of these figures is no longer frontal and linear: there is a strong feeling of volume and the beginning of torso articulation and motion.

The Hōryūji murals

The most magnificent examples of late Hakuhō painting are the murals of the rebuilt Hōryūji Golden Hall. The murals are over 3 metres high; the four large central ones measure 2.5 metres across and the eight corner ones 1.8 metres. They are a very rare example of mural painting: this may have been the first time a monastery was so decorated. (The usual wall-decoration in Buddhist halls, before and since, was hangings of painted, woven or embroidered silk.) The Golden Hall was completed some time between 680 and 690, and the murals finished by around 711.

The artisans, of immigrant Chinese and Korean descent, had been organized into craft guilds responsible for the decoration of palaces and temples. The Taihō-ryō decree of 701 established a Painters' Bureau (*edakumi-no-tsukasa*) under the Ministry of Internal Affairs, and was presided over by three civil officials. The bureau had four master-painters (*eshi*) and sixty ordinary painters (*edakumi*) living in the metropolitan area, and several groups of private painters living in the provinces (*sato-eshi*) who could be summoned to the capital for large-scale projects. The institution of official painters continued to exist in some form or other for another thousand years, until the Meiji restoration of 1868.

To make the murals, the Kondō wall surface was first covered with a layer of fine white clay. Then the artisan transferred the design from a pouncing pattern using a fine even red or ink line, then added colours including cinnabar, red ochre and red lead for the reds, ochre and litharge for yellow, malachite for green and azurite for blue. The figures have the same sensuous and fleshy presence as Chinese High Tang painting of the period, such as those in the Dunhuang caves dating to 642 and 698 AD, with the bodies slightly twisted and relaxed in *tribhanga* or *contraposto* pose which separates the planes of torso, upper and lower abdomen and places the weight on one leg, with the other slightly lifted in motion. The most famous of the figures is perhaps the Kannon (Avalokiteśvara) in the Amida Paradise on the West Wall. Full, sensuous lips and long, deep-set eyes are vestigial traces of its Indian and Khotan sources and, still more distant in time and space, of ancient Greece. The magnificent presence of the deity is captured with firm technical assurance. The stylistic relationship with the bodhisattva line drawing on the door panels of the Lady

33

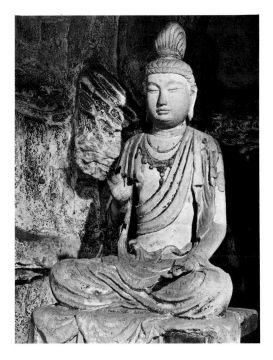

30 Bodhisattva Monjū from Hōryūji Pagoda. Clay. H. 50.9 cm. Early Tempyō, 711.

Tachibana Shrine is unmistakable, suggesting variant pouncing patterns from the same source. When the Kondō was completed the effect of the Paradise images, flanked by bodhisattvas, and with apsaras flying overhead in prayerful attitudes, must have been resplendent and inspiring. When the Shaka Triad for the original Kondō was moved in, it must have seemed odd, being much too small for the enlarged hall and by now in a very antiquated style.

Buddhism and centralized power

When Prince Shōtoku embraced Chinese statecraft and Buddhism, he had envisioned the first, based on Confucian ethics, as underpinning the whole administrative and penal system; Buddhism remained for him a private personal faith. Church and state did not finally converge, so to speak, until over a century later, in the person of Emperor Shōmu (reigned 724–749). In 741 Shōmu launched a massive building programme of Buddhist monasteries and temples throughout the land, ostensibly for the protection of the nation, but also as a compelling monument to his own imperial authority. (To do this in fact ran counter to the basic tenets of Buddhism, which aims at the salvation of the individual soul, sees no class distinctions and is universally benevolent.) The new monasteries were created and served by massive labour conscriptions which recruited untold numbers of the nation's population, including slave groups, to the service of the central government. Buddhist monks were no longer free to preach the sūtras as they saw fit, nor were monks and nuns permitted to hold religious observances on unauthorized premises. The clergy in effect were now licensed by the government.

Tempyō religious art: the Tōdaiji 752

In 743 Emperor Shōmu vowed to cast a massive Rushana Buddha (Universal Light, Vairocana); the project was properly begun in 745. All the copper in the land was commandeered for the massive statue which towered over 14 metres high; Japanese bronze-casting thereafter ceased for centuries. The Great Buddha symbolized the dominance of Buddhism and its spread among the populace. It was no longer a private faith for the leisured and learned but a protection for the land and all its people.

The Tōdaiji project exacted a huge toll in money and labour. An estimated ten per cent of the populace, down to the poorest beggars, contributed in some way or another; there were 50,000 carpenters and over 370,000 metal smiths. The casting was begun in Shōmu's palace grounds in Shigaraki; but after numerous failures the site was changed to Nara in 745 and the work was completed after four more years. The largest wooden structure in the world was built around it; its front of eleven bays was some 73 metres across and tied into a cloister of 154 bays. Its proportions and roof pitch may have roughly resembled that of the Shōsōin repository which is one of three storehouses among the numerous structures in the original compound. Twin pagodas, three times the height of the Hōryūji Pagoda, soared 100 metres into the air. With its numerous gates, halls and sub-temples, the Tōdaiji compound is the largest in Japan and dominated the new capital of Heijō (Nara). In a spectacular ceremony, attended by every member of court and the clergy, the monastery and Great Buddha of Nara were dedicated in 752. But in the half century that followed, its power proved too much for the government which was forced to seek yet another site for the capital.

The Great Buddha of Nara we see today has been reworked several times and the Buddha Hall is a reduced and squared-off version of its once magnificent proportions. For a glimpse of the original Great Buddha, in all the splendour of gold-leaf gilt, we must resort to two slightly later works, and to an early painted illustration. Both statues were made in dry

31 Head of Fukūkenjaku
Kannon in the Sangatsudō.
Gilded dry lacquer. H. 360.3
cm. 746.

lacquer, no more copper being available. The Fukūkenjaku Kannon of   31
746 is the main statue in Tōdaiji's Hokkedo (Lotus Hall) sub-temple,
commonly called the Sangatsudō (Third Month Hall). It stands nearly 4
metres tall, and is probably the work of the sculptors responsible for the
Great Buddha, headed by Kuni-naka Muraji Kimimaro. It is an eight-
armed bodhisattva whose third left hand holds a rope to symbolize the
hunting and fishing for salvation of souls. As the bodhisattva towers over
a high wooden pedestal, its majestic, serene face is usually missed by
viewers. The cheeks and chin are full but not heavy; the long, slanted eyes
are modelled with curved upper lids which give them a gentle, loving
expression beneath arched and bevelled brows. A vertical third eye is
partially open in the forehead and a black pearl decorates the spot between
the brows. The mouth is modulated and full, with upper and lower lips in
symmetrical M and W shapes which echo the curves of the rest of the face.
The elaborate silver crown is encrusted with thousands of precious stones,
pearl, agate and crystals, and is swathed with chains holding carved beads
in the antique *magatama* shape. A twenty-centimetre silver Amida Buddha
stands in the middle, hands spread in the *mūdra* of bestowing peace of
mind. Although the Kannon clearly reflects Tang features, the Amida's
face shows vestigial traces of the Koguryō mien, in the eyes and two sharp
points rising in the centre of the upper lip.

The other statue which may indicate some original features of the Great
Buddha is in the Golden Hall (Kondō) of Tōshōdaiji, west of Nara. It is a

32   seated Vairocana or Rushana Buddha, 4 metres high, and was made of gilded dry lacquer in 759. An elaborate aureole originally had one thousand seated Buddhas on thirty-two clusters, most of which are still in place. The Rushana Buddha's face is more heavy-set than that of the Sangatsudō Kannon and the neck-folds are modelled around a dropped chin. The eyes look down from under thick, curved lids, and slant to the nose in an expression more severe than compassionate, more lordly than tender. The original Great Buddha of Tōdaiji was designed to be Emperor Shōmu's symbol of state and may well have combined the qualities of these two works, a severe but benevolent colossus which radiated

34   protective light over the land. From a twelfth century handscroll we can deduce still more of its architectural details and emotional impact. In a time-sequenced vignette, like those of the Tamamushi Shrine *jātaka*, a pilgrim nun is shown several times during her night at Tōdaiji. The colossal, gilt-bronze Buddha towers benignly over her as she prays for divine guidance. The eleven bays have slatted door-panels which open inwards and seem taller than the four-square door-panels of today's

32 Rushana Buddha, in Tōshōdaiji. Gilded dry lacquer. H. 303 cm. 759.

33 Kannon from the Amida Paradise on the Hōryūji murals. 711. (Damaged by fire in 1949.)

48

reduced edifice of seven bays. The total impression of the old building was horizontal, not square, and the impact of the statue must have been more immediate when it was placed, as illustrated here, squarely in the middle of the space with little to hinder the spectator's view.

The Japanese and continental influences

At this point we should perhaps consider the remarkable speed with which the Japanese assimilated continental cultural stimuli, particularly Buddhism. It was not a matter of sudden and overwhelming direct or indirect contact; there had been frequent contacts for millennia. Massive cultural receptivity in the Asuka period, therefore, may reflect a new Japanese realization of national inadequacy in the face of an urbane, continental culture and a compensatory urgent desire for international respectability. In the Tempyō period, the Japanese whole-heartedly adopted Chinese culture, Buddhism and statecraft. Administrative and court rituals were regulated on continental models; court wear changed from Korean to Chinese; palaces were built in continental style with tiled roofs, bright crimson pillars and slate floors.

All these imports were, however, no more than an external covering draped over a Japanese framework. Not all parts fitted. The original mammoth Great Buddha Hall of Tōdaiji, for example, based as it was on Chinese imperial scale, and requiring the removal of entire hills to provide the site, must have been drastically out of proportion with the surrounding Yamato hills. In spite of the new regard for external prestige, when it came to personal habits, native preferences remained strong. In particular, Chinese food and eating habits were rejected; later, even within the Chinese-style palace compound in Heian-kyō, the Emperor's private quarters (*dairi*) retained the Japanese traditions of cedar-bark roofs and pillars of plain, undecorated wood.

35, 36 The same contrast can be seen in the Tōshōdaiji Kondō and Kōdō built in the latter half of the eighth century. The Kondō shows Chinese solidity, symmetry and grandeur. (Its present roof soars some fifteen feet higher than the original, however, destroying the previous impact of power and vigour.) Across the court stands the Lecture Hall (Kōdō) whose simplicity and horizontality, stressed by the slender pillars, are typical examples of japanization. Originally part of the Heijō Palace, it was donated to Tōshōdaiji and moved there in the late eighth century when the fortunes of that monastery waned. Although now tiled, the ridge is extended to run nearly the entire length of the roof (a Shintō characteristic) and is gabled at each end to soften the drop of the eaves.

34 Tōdaiji scene showing the Great Buddha in the *Shigisan Engi*. Narrative handscroll. 12th century.

Even in the face of persistent continental influence, such examples of indigenous traits persevered. It is obviously possible to import major aspects of another people's material culture but it is not possible simultaneously to import every one of its social and spiritual attitudes. (The same situation exists today, where an intensive effort is made to assert Japan's 'International Image' in the art world. Artists with an 'international image' are sent to exhibitions abroad but those who create works uninfluenced by the large world, however accomplished and original, are ignored at home and excluded from publicity abroad.) This desire for parity with external powers may have its genesis in the Tempyō period of self discovery and self assessment.

The Tōshōdaiji is a major symbol of the reforms instigated by Emperor Shōmu. He felt that the Buddhist clergy of the time had become too lax and sent Japanese monks to China to find a leader who would purify and

35 Kondō (Golden Hall) of Tōshōdaiji. Tang style. Late 8th century. (Roof has since been raised.)

36 Kōdō (Lecture Hall) of Tōshōdaiji, more Japanese in its horizontal emphasis. Late 8th century.

37 Ganjin seated in meditation. Dry lacquer.
H. 79.7 cm. Late 8th century.

revitalize religious practice. After years of searching they found Master
Ganjin (Jianzhen in Chinese) who, when his disciples showed unwilling-
ness to travel such distances to an undeveloped land, took on the mission
himself. At the age of sixty-seven, in 753, he arrived in Japan after a
disastrous seven year journey, during which he was blinded. In 762,
Ganjin ordained a group of monks and nuns in the courtyard of Tōdaiji,
in the presence of the Emperor and the imperial court.

A remarkable dry lacquer sculpture of the time shows the aged and   37
learned Master Ganjin in profound meditation. The naturalistic depiction
of such physical features as the blind eyes, the mouth resolute yet kind and
the aged but firm cheeks and chin, is matched by the extraordinary
expression of emotion and spirituality. This combination of realism and
expressiveness in sculpture was to become one of Japan's major contributions to world art.

Tempyō secular art

In 756, Emperor Shōmu's widow dedicated all his treasures to the Great
Buddha. They are still in the Shōsōin repository of the Tōdaiji monastery
and give a lively and detailed picture of court life in the first half of the

38 Ink painting of entertainers on a long bow. Lacquer on catalpa wood. L. 162 cm. From Emperor Shōmu's treasure, before 756.

39 Knives in Persian-style jewelled, silver scabbards, with a dedicatory tag by Shōmu's widow. 8th century.

eighth century. There were imperial clothing, prayer beads, swords and ornaments; musical instruments such as lutes, flutes, the double-reeded *xiao* and *sheng*, the transverse flute and the plucked string instrument called *qin* in Chinese; board games such as *go*; bows, arrows, quivers, armour and saddles. Inner chambers were hung with textiles and furnished with mirrors, standing screens, portable shrines, masks for musical performances, baskets, cabinets, flower vases and hanging incense-burners, brushes and writing tools. Examples of calligraphy by the Emperor, the Empress and after the Chinese 'Sage of Calligraphy' Wang Xizhi (303–379) were also dedicated and are preserved to this day.

38, 39

Many of these objects are of native manufacture and their motifs and materials reflect an assimilation of diverse influences. Glass ware suggests Mediterranean origins; objects of tooled gold and silver, adorned with Persian motifs, are similar to the cache buried near Xian, the Tang capital in 756 (and excavated in 1970). Silk and hemp are woven, or resist-dyed, in symmetrical patterns in the manner of Persian hangings. Elaborately inlaid and evenly distributed designs on lacquer objects ranging from boxes to lutes are signs of Central Asian influence. Whereas the Chinese were happy to accept such foreign influence throughout imperial history, their presence here is a short-lived phenomenon. Although Chinese artists accepted all kinds of Central Asian, Indian and Persian influences and continued for several generations to produce works in the cosmopolitan amalgam known as the Tang style; in Japan the Tang fad seems to have lasted less than three generations. Almost none of Shōmu's imported styles found a place in subsequent arts.

Amid the new and exotic influences on the objects in the Shōsōin, there are clear indications of native Japanese discrimination, i.e. selection and rejection. A good example is the mother-of-pearl inlaid Chinese lute, 40 called a Genkan (*Ruan Xian*) after the Chinese musician of that name. It is decorated with a pair of pearly pink parrots flying in a circle round a central medallion of kaleidoscopic and radiating roundels. The form of this instrument and the Middle Eastern technique of mother-of-pearl inlay became part of Japanese tradition, but the roundel motif and symmetry had gone by the next generation.

40 *Ruan Xian* (4-stringed lute) (detail). Wood with mother-of-pearl inlay. Early 7th century.

41 Covered medicine jar. Ash-glazed clay. H. 18.5 cm. An inscription dates it to 811.

42 Plectrum guard of *biwa* lute. Shitan wood decorated with marquetry and painted. 756.

43 Map of Tōdaiji precincts (detail). Light colours on hemp. (North is at the bottom.) Note the *Yamato-e*-like hills in contrast with Chinese pinnacles of pl. 42. 756.

41   In another example, an early ninth-century ash-glazed pot from the Shōsōin repository, while fairly centred and well formed (according to Tang canons) is glazed naturally by the falling ash settling on the shoulders, producing a mottled and uneven transparent green glaze. The Chinese potter would have considered such a glaze imperfect, even unacceptable; the Japanese saw in it another dimension of beauty. The potter neither controls nor wishes to control every inch of the surface decoration and lets both the material and the firing process play a part in the finished work. Although ninth-century Japanese potters did make Tang-style 'three-colour' (Tang *sancai*) glazed wares, these found little

favour with later generations. By contrast, later natural-glazed Japanese pottery, such as Tamba and Bizen wares, achieved worldwide renown and clearly show the potters' awareness of the beauty of the so-called 'accident'.

Over ten thousand objects were donated to the Great Buddha of Tōdaiji during the eighth and early ninth centuries by the court. It is a treasure house of the arts to be found along the Silk Road which linked China to the Mediterranean, and offers the present-day observer clear examples of those styles which Japanese artists accepted, rejected or modified. Another example is the painting (which shows clear Chinese influence) on the plectrum guard of a *biwa* lute. Two gentlemen have paused momentarily, one in the midst of writing, to gaze upon the cliff to the left and are lost in a state of communion with nature. The image has faded; only drawings made from infra-red photography now reveal the basic outlines. The scene is typically Tang, with the emphasis on awesome, beetling scenery. The peaks are adorned with trees, their ornamental forms spread out against the sky and cliffs. The painting is fluid, with few straight lines or harsh forms, and successfully suggests harmony between the two watching figures and the natural scene.

A large map of the precincts of Tōdaiji, painted in 756, offers another glimpse of how knowledge of Chinese landscape painting was used. The sharply rising cliffs of the previous example are here replaced by gently

42

43

rolling hillocks like those of the Yamato plains. (These gentle outlines later became the hallmark of native Yamato-e painting.) The trees on top of the hills do not pierce the sky like those on the *biwa* plectrum and are rendered by thick ink lines in soft curves. They do not cover the entire hill but are scattered irregularly over the central portions. On the Chinese-style plectrum painting the trees are evenly spaced in a Middle Eastern manner, whereas the Tōdaiji map disperses the elements in an irregular and natural manner. The map incidentally shows us the main buildings of Tōdaiji in 756: two L-shaped red brackets show the front of the Main or Great Buddha Hall; two squarish ink outlines at the sides are the East and West Pagodas, already a clear change from the Hōryūji plan which had only one pagoda. To the east, a Chinese building with tiled roof and four posts on a platform, is the Senjūdō or Thousand Armed Kannon Hall. The Kaidanin or Ordination Hall is indicated to the north-west.

Chinese figure painting had two main styles, one for the more formal, portrait-like images and the other less formal, showing people following natural pursuits. Whereas Chinese figures tended increasingly towards psychic introversion and tranquillity so that characters in a common situation show little interest in each other, in Japan the reverse seems true. Here figures and motifs reach out toward each other physically or psychologically. Portraits are relegated largely to religious painting.

An example of the impressive style is the set of deftly painted ink figures on the inside of a bow with ninety-six acrobats, jugglers, musicians and dancers caught in mid-action. Their faces reveal different personalities and moods. The strong man balancing four children on top of his head stands with eyes closed in concentration, while the children look warily down. The man balancing four other children on a cross-barred pole has just taken a step; his effort is clearly visible. While the children show absorption in what they are doing, the onlookers express emotions which range from curiosity to concern. Lower down, musicians accompany a dance. The artist has exploited the narrowness of the format by diagonally linking the last person on one group with the first person of the next by eye contact. The development of this style was carried to extraordinarily expressive heights in the succeeding Heian period.

38

CHAPTER FOUR

Heian (794–1185)

Towards national identity: the new capital and new Buddhism

The imposition of Chinese institutions upon Japanese society was too swift and widespread and proved unworkable. The Confucian system of statecraft required learning centres with examinations, designed to foster a democratic meritocracy. A Japanese National University was founded, with about four hundred students in the capital and fifty in each regional centre. However, entrants were restricted to the hereditary aristocracy and examination administration was lax. The entrenched interests of the regional nobility prevented the proper functioning of a government built upon ethical practice. High-minded Confucian scholars often called for reforms, but their memoranda carried little weight with an idle and aristocratic class.

The great monasteries grew to unwieldy proportions. Tōdaiji, for example, once owned more than 12,000 tax-exempt acres, burdening farmers and impoverishing the national treasury. The monks of Nara were cosmopolitan and worldly, and often involved themselves in Court intrigues, to the detriment of proper administration. In China, the government had occasionally suppressed Buddhism, even persecuting the Church in order to defend its own authority. The Japanese solution was quite different: in 784 Emperor Kammu and his court fled from Nara. After several abortive attempts to settle in Nagaoka, in 793 work began on the site for an entirely new capital. This was called Heian-Kyō (Capital of Peace and Tranquillity), present day Kyoto, which remained the seat of the imperial court until the Meiji Restoration of 1868. Significantly, the great monasteries remained in Nara.

The establishment of a new capital ushered in an era based on the newly introduced Buddhist principles, which stressed inner spiritual discipline unhindered by mundane considerations. Two great religious leaders, Saichō and Kūkai, established schools of Buddhism which were to have lasting effects on Japanese life.

Saichō (767–822) grew up under Chinese monks in Nara. He disliked the spreading decadence and spiritual laxity among the clergy there, however, and left to found a small monastery on Mount Hiei. (Small mountain retreats were common in Chinese Taoism and Buddhism.) When Emperor Kammu arrived at Heian-Kyō he found Saichō already practising a systematic spiritual discipline nearby. According to Chinese geomancy, the mountain was the *kimon* or demon entrance to the capital; hence Saichō's presence protected the city. Reverences he paid to the gods of Mount Hiei, in a genial amalgam of Buddhism and Shintō practices, were thought to assure the city. Kammu was impressed by Saichō's rigorous discipline and in 804 sent him to study in China. When Saichō returned, a year later, he brought back new learning from Mount Tiantai.

The Tiantai School was a native Chinese development – that is, without Indian precedent – which sought to reconcile all aspects of Buddhist doctrine in a single discipline, and, significantly, to provide solace for the common man. Salvation was no longer the prerogative of the rich or learned, and would not be achieved exclusively by scriptural study, charitable works or religious practices, but from a dedicated combination of all three. Saichō advocated the reading of the Lotus Sutra (subsequently one of the most influential texts in Japanese Buddhism). It assured the salvation not only of men, but also of women, and stressed the importance of the arts.

Licensed by the Emperor, Saichō founded the Tendai Lotus School on Mount Hiei. In time it became a national centre of culture and learning, with some 300 buildings spread over the summit and flanks of the mountain. A connection with the court was prominent from the outset, and continued until the monastery was destroyed in 1571. Kammu was a Confucian by training and was impressed by Saichō's moral calibre; Saichō, for his part, was extremely loyal to the throne, even requiring his monks to swear an oath which included a moving declaration of indebtedness to Kammu. This was a major step in the japanization of Buddhism.

The second leader was the brilliant master Kūkai (774–835). He excelled as a spiritual leader and as a calligrapher, poet, scholar, inventor and explorer. Born into an aristocratic family, he showed remarkable intellectual precocity. At the age of seventeen he wrote a treatise analysing the teachings of Confucianism, Buddhism and Taoism; revised in 797, it remains a major theoretical work. In 804 he sailed to China to study with the great Huiguo (746–805). On his return, in 806, Saichō begged him for lessons. In 816 he built a monastery on Mt Kōya, establishing the Shingon (True Word or Mantra) School of esoteric Buddhism, a system whose mysteries, including the True Words themselves, were taught privately, orally and directly, and were never written down. In 822 he was

44 Womb Mandala (detail), showing Tibetan influence. Ink, colours on silk. Heian, 859–880.

appointed Abbot of Kyōōgokokuji, Monastery for the Salvation of the Emperor and Protection of the Realm, called Tōji for short, the great East Temple commanding the main entrance to the capital.

Shingon and the Mandalas

The teachings of Shingon focus on the essential unity of the noumenal and the phenomenal (or the spiritual and the physical worlds). These are represented by painted or sculpted illustrations of the Diamond and Womb Mandalas respectively, the universe of Dainichi Nyorai (Great Sun or Mahāvairocana), greatest of all Buddhas. The mystery and aestheticism of Shingon held great appeal for Heian courtiers. From their rich colours and schemata spring many subsequent formulae in Buddhist art.

The Womb (phenomenal) World is represented by a series of concentric squares, the innermost of which contains an eight-petalled red lotus with a Buddha sitting on each petal. As Yanagisawa Taka has shown, the mandala here illustrated is one of the earliest Shingon polychrome mandalas painted in Japan; it is a copy of the pair commissioned by Emperor Montoku and produced in Tang Changan under the supervision of the prelate Faquan and painter Diaoqing, and brought back to Japan by the Japanese monk Enchin in 859 AD. They retain the strong shading and high colour contrast typical of Tibetan painting – following Buddhist persecutions Changan had to replace its Buddhist texts and art from Dunhuang caves which had been under Tibetan occupation between 786 and 843 – but otherwise show several signs of japanization, of departure from the Sino-Tibetan model: in particular, the way in which the faces of the deities exhibit a variety of expressions and look in different directions is indicative of an interest in individual particularities which appears in subsequent Japanese Buddhist art involving groups of apsaras, attendants or worshippers. Dainichi Nyorai is in the centre; the bodhisattvas Myō-ō (Acalas), Ten (Devas) and other deities are ranked, in decreasing size, about the central square. The Mandala of the Diamond (noumenal) World has nine equal-sized square mandalas forming a single large square. The believer's task was to contemplate aspects of the mandalas and by means of such meditation and other rites, to realize Buddhahood in this human realm.

Kūkai designed his monastic buildings to conform with the plan of the mandalas. The sculptures are arranged in schematic form and the two pagodas are representations of the Diamond and Womb Mandalas. Specific areas of the mandalas come within the groundplan of the pagodas.

Jōgan Sculpture

The new sculptures of this era are dark and heavy, with an air of mystery and inward absorption, but so powerful as to seem forbidding. The 'Jōgan style', actually named after the reign era between 859 and 877, is used to designate all the heavy-set, brooding sculptures of the early Heian period. Many large works are carved from single blocks of Japanese cypress, and Indian and Tang (Chinese) influences are marked. A typical example is the awesome Yakushi Nyorai of Jingoji in Kyoto. The massive, 47 elongated head reveals powerful chisel marks around sharply bevelled features of forbidding power and severity. Intentionally larger than life, the neck is stylized (three rings of equal size), and the shoulders are four-square and high. The symmetrical folds of the drapery are intended to focus the viewer's attention, inducing concentration as if by hypnosis.

More conservative is the magnificent Shaka Norai, central image of the Murōji in Nara. The figure is also markedly fleshy, the torso broad, solid 48 and powerful. But the face is related to late eighth-century style such as that of the Fukūkenjaku Kannon in the Hokkedō of Tōdaiji in Nara. The 31 sensuous mouth, rounded chin and high, arched eyebrows radiate compassion and benevolence; the expression is outgoing and welcoming, in marked contrast to that of the Jingoji Yakushi.

The Shingon School found room not only for Indian deities but for indigenous Shintō gods as well. From the start of the Heian period, Shintō shrines appear within Buddhist monastery compounds and Buddhist buildings in Shintō precincts. Shintō deities were identified as local manifestations of Shingon's universal truth, and were represented alongside Buddhist icons. As time went on, Shintō began to lose its identity and became a convenient intermediary between the new religion and the native population.

One of the major deities in Shingon teaching, Fudō Myō-ō (Acalanā- 46 tha, the King of Light), is widely depicted in painting and sculpture. As a bringer of light and wisdom, he was a popular household icon, particularly as his spectacular powers could be invoked by prayer. He looked ferocious, with protruding teeth, glowering eyes and furrowed brow, poised amid billowing flames holding a double-edged sword in his right hand and a lassoo in his left; no earthly evil could match him.

The glowing world of Pure Land Buddhism

Sir George Sansom characterized late Heian culture as a 'rule of taste' which extended into nearly every facet of daily life and made 'religion into an art and art into a religion'. An outstanding example of this is the belief

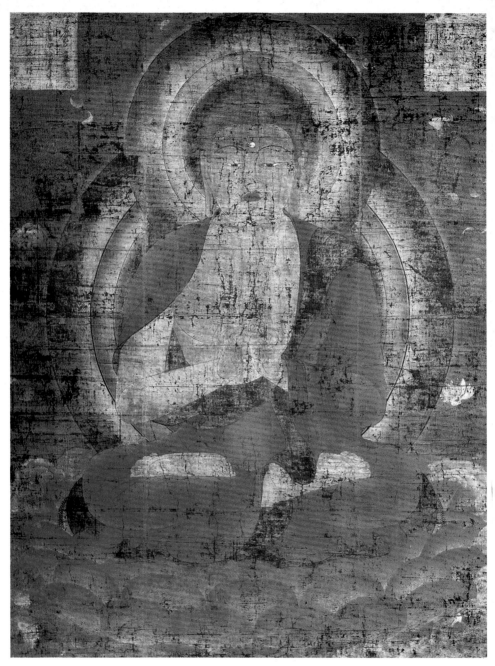

45 Amida on a cloud, the central panel of the Amida triptych. Colours on silk. Early 11th century.

46 Shingon deity Blue Fudō and his *dōji* attendants. Colours on silk. Mid-11th century.

47 Yakushi Nyorai. Painted cypress wood. Early 9th century.

48 Shaka Nyorai. Painted wood. Late 9th century.

in Amida's Western Pure Land Paradise, a belief which inspired some of the most beautiful art traditions of Japan. This was largely due to the Tendai priest Kūya (903–72) and to the pilgrimages he made all over Japan. He was called 'the Amida saint' because of his *nembutsu*, a ceaseless recitation of the name of Amida, Buddha of the Western Paradise. (Of the four basic types of meditation, *nembutsu*, thanks to Kūya's proselytizing example, became that chiefly practised by the laity: Amida's name was soon on everyone's lips.)

Another Amidist leader, Genshin (942–1017), recommended a dying nobleman on a distant frontier to intone Amida's name while fixing his eyes on a *raigō-zu* (a picture of the Amida Buddha welcoming the new soul to Paradise). This practice become widespread, and resulted in a dramatic increase in *raigō* paintings throughout Japan. Like the Fudō-ō, the *raigō* was originally one of the subsidiary scenes from the mandalas. Now it became important as an object of contemplation, inspiring works of great beauty in a new and distinctly Japanese pictorial style.

66

45 One of the earliest and most sublime *raigō* paintings is the central panel of the Amida triptych in Hokkeji in Nara. The composition is symmetrical and frontal. Amida's eyes gaze directly downwards at the beholder, as if to draw his soul up into the Pure Land Paradise. The ethereal quality is enhanced by gradual, high contrast shading of the lotus petals and the aureole. The Amida is rendered in sure and sensitive lines and simple colours. Discreet dark red swastikas pattern the robe and delicate green shading beneath the eyebrows lends an aristocratic air. The style of the face and the close colour harmony are strongly Japanese. This luminous and transparent image absorbs the believer with a quiet mystery and magnetism.

The Fujiwara period (897–1185)

By the end of the ninth century, Shōtoku's bureaucracy of the meritorious had virtually vanished. The emperor's function was merely to preside over fossilized state rituals, and actual power went into the hands of the regent (*sesshō*) and chancellor (*kampaku*). From the mid-ninth century onwards, Japan was ruled by the powerful Fujiwara clan, who strengthened their position by regularly marrying their daughters into the enfeebled imperial family. Government schools, originally meant to train future civil servants, were only open to those of court rank, descendants from clans close to the Yamato ruling family. Courtiers amassed vast wealth from grants of land; conspicuous consumption accompanied rank and prestige. The new ruling class had regained those powers held prior to the seventh century reforms. In time, courtiers in the capital became an élite, far superior to their provincial equivalents. Late Heian culture was centred on the capital and dominated by the Fujiwara family. For the next millenium, the role of emperor was that of a figurehead.

The Phoenix Hall

The regent Fujiwara Yorimichi (994–1074) demonstrated his power and influence by converting his residence into a copy of the Pure Land Paradise itself, as represented in the Taima Mandala, imported from China in the late ninth century. The exquisite park in Uji, outside Kyoto,
49 is a perfect setting for the *Byōdōin*, his private chapel, completed in 1053. With its harmonious fusion of religious fervour and aristocratic splendour, the Byōdōin itself is the ultimate expression of the age.

Fujiwara Yorimichi's master sculptor was Jōchō, whose father Kōshō had worked for Yorimichi's father, Fujiwara no Michinaga (966–1027).

49 View of Byōdōin, in Uji, Kyoto, showing front portico. Completed 1053.

The conversion of the Fujiwara estate into the *Byōdōin* Pure Land Paradise both introduced and consolidated several aspects of japanization. Its main building, the Phoenix Hall, for example, is not of colossal proportions but is built on a human scale, at once enveloping the Amida figure with intimacy and warmth and achieving characteristic Fujiwara clarity and airiness. Although Chinese-style tiles, pillars and whitewashed walls remain, the raised angle of the eaves, enhanced by the reflection in the surrounding water, gives an impression of imminent, graceful flight.

The Amida Hall (today called the Phoenix Hall because of the phoenixes crowning its rooftop) was built on a small island in the middle of an artificial lake. The central image of Amida, of gilded and lacquered 52 joined woodblocks, is 2.5 metres high, and is seated on a golden lotus in *dhyānamudrā* of concentration or absorption. It is considered Jōchō's masterpiece. Its proportions are those of the perfect human ideal: the rounded head, poised on a graceful neck, is balanced by gently sloping shoulders and softly articulated knees. The awesome mystery of Jōgan sculpture gives way to mercy and compassion. The deity is approachable; the chapel envelops one in a feeling of intimacy, of earthly aspiration raised to sublime and lyrical heights.

On entering the Phoenix Hall, the visitor's gaze is immediately drawn to the shining Amida, and then upwards to the dazzling openwork

50 (*left*) *Raigō* of *Amida and Celestial Host* (detail) from a Phoenix Hall mural. Colours on wood, 1053.

51 (*below*) Celestial bodhisattva on a cloud, school of Jōchō, from the background of pl. 52. Painted wood. Heian, 1053.

52 (*opposite*) Jōchō's masterpiece, the Buddha Amida. Gold leaf and lacquer on wood. H. 295 cm. 1053.

canopy which is gilded, lacquered and inlaid with mother-of-pearl. The entire ceiling consists of elaborately painted and latticed woodwork. Behind the Amida is a flame-like golden aureole, adorned with gilded flying apsaras in worshipful attitudes. On the walls, murals show the Western Pure Land Paradise in four seasons, with descending Amida *raigō* and attendants coming to receive the soul of the faithful. On the south door is a particularly striking *raigō* image of *Amida and the Celestial Host*. It shows Amida gazing down at an unseen soul in the lower right of the painting. His hands are in the *mudrā* of welcome (the right thumb and forefinger joined and the hand raised up, while the open left hand is extended downward towards the dying believer). The mural depicts not only a host of celestial beings playing musical instruments and monks

51

50

53 *Suiten* (Water Deva), one of twelve. Colours and gold on silk. 1127.

absorbed in prayer, but also (a new element, reflecting national taste) Japan's rural landscape – the serene, lowlying hillocks and meandering streams of Yamato. The reassuring familiarity and ethereal clarity of these images suited the new *nembutsu* Amidist practice far better than the complexity of the earlier Shingon school.

Above the murals, over the whitewashed upper register of the walls, fifty-two monks and bodhisattvas descend on clouds. In high relief, they are dancing, playing instruments and praying. The great variety of mid-eleventh-century sculptural techniques is clearly visible, as only small traces of gilt and paint remain. The most advanced technique is used for the central figure of Amida. Single-block sculptures of great size had been found to split, wrap and crack, even if the core had been hollowed. Jōchō and his craftsmen prevented this by revolutionary *yosegi* and *warihagi* techniques where the main block was cut into front and back halves, hollowed and rejoined for carving. Additional pieces were added to the sides, back and front where necessary. These techniques ensured strength and stability and were favoured through the Kamakura period. They also enabled Jōchō and his workshop to mass-produce Buddhist sculpture in assembly line fashion. The School prospered and one branch later moved to Nara where it produced the Kei School of sculptors in the Kamakura period.

Very much in the manner of the Jōchō School are the endearing *gokuraku* or paradise sculptures made in 1094 for the Sokujōji monastery in Kyoto. They were sculpted from Japanese cypress in the multi-block technique, then lacquered and gilded. An extra fifteen attendants were added to the original ten during the Edo period. Here the bodhisattva Kannon (Avalokiteśvara) is kneeling forward, holding a lotus pedestal to receive the newly ascending soul. 54

The effects of court taste are even more pronounced in twelfth-century art. The perception of celestial beings, such as the Water Deva (*Suiten*), one of the twelve in Tōji, for example, closely reflects courtly ideals. 53 Their expressions are aristocratic and dream-like. Compared to the robust Devas charged with the protection of the realm in the ninth-century *Womb Mandala*, the stress is clearly on aesthetics, and less on spirituality. Compared to the Hokkeji Amida of the early eleventh century with its diaphanous luminescence, the Water Deva is even more gorgeous and more sensuous, and the use of many more layers of colour allows for subtler colour-harmonies and contrast. The impression of absorption given by the earlier image is here replaced by one of beatific tranquillity.

Kamakura Buddhist painting of the thirteenth century shows a new spiritual vigour. There is a new *raigō* form showing Amida and his

54 *Raigō* Kannon Bosatsu, one of twenty-five figures. Gold leaf and lacquer on wood. H. 96.7 cm. 1094.

55 *Descent of Amida over the Mountains.* Hanging scroll; colours and gold on silk. Kamakura, early 13th century.

55   attendants, two or more, appearing over the mountains. Amida looms over the landscape, as if parting the hills and coming directly towards the viewer. Kannon (right) and Seishi (left) are standing on clouds in reverential and welcoming positions, flanked by the Four Celestial Kings and the Two Children in hierarchically reduced scale. The landscape is relatively realistic but the superimposition of the heavenly host is dramatically out of scale, compelling, immediate and immanent. The sweetness of the Water Deva, and the innocence of the Jōchō images are here superceded by an alert spirituality, simple and vigorous. The Yamato landscape is quickened with a sense of urgency.

56   In *The descent of Amida and his host* (popularly known as *Haya Raigō* or 'rapid descent'), the Buddha Amida and twenty-five bodhisattvas on a white cloud are descending at a steep angle above a precipitous mountain towards the priest below, who sits upright at the very moment of death. This is an example of the painting style known as *kubon raigō-zu* (Nine

74

56 *Haya raigō* of Amida and bodhisattvas. Hanging scroll; colours and gold on silk. Kamakura, 13th century.

grades of Amitabha's descent), of which we have seen an earlier (mid-eleventh-century) example in the Phoenix Hall mural. Comparison at once shows the increased urgency of the later work. The Paradise itself, usually the focus of gorgeous achitectural painting, is here reduced to a palace in the upper right corner; instead, the landscape of *this* life looms large. The figures are all standing, their attention focussed on the new soul. Gold is liberally used and the lacy intricacy of Heian decoration here gives way to flat application of unmixed pigment. The landscape is sombre and vertiginous compared to that of the Phoenix Hall; emphasis has shifted from an idyllic conception of Paradise to the moment of rebirth itself; dream has given way to action.

Fujiwara secular arts

In their secular arts, although Heian courtiers enjoyed Chinese poetry and painting, indigenous production, even when in the Chinese manner, increasingly showed Japanese qualities. In 894, as the much admired Chinese Tang dynasty was disintegrating and voyages to China were fraught with danger, the Japanese court decided to stop diplomatic missions altogether. This isolation served to trigger an unparalleled outpouring of Japanese splendours.

Like its Chinese counterpart (Northern Song, 960–1126), this late Heian or Fujiwara period (897–1185) was one of introspection and self discovery. Both cultures were settling down after the ebullient and extrovert phases of Tang and Nara. During those cosmopolitan centuries, both China and Japan had been flushed with the power of newly consolidated realms. Japan had assimilated a host of spiritual and visual stimuli which had swept from Central Asia, India and Sassanian Persia. In the tenth and eleventh centuries, however, both the Song and Heian cultures turned inward; political unassertiveness enabled them to discover their aesthetic identity and release the unfolding of their greatest artistic glory. Song China produced landscape painting and the Heian court *Yamato-e*. At this time, Japan's own calligraphic form, *kana* writing, also reached its zenith. And the profound differences between the two cultures became manifest; in Japan, many aesthetic preferences which were to become hallmarks of Japanese art now found full expression. (Curiously enough, however, the subdued colour tone, the use of bird's-eye perspective and the frequent stress of the diagonal have all been traced back to Song sources.)

The growing apart of the two cultures can be seen in a comparison of painting techniques. In Northern Song, the flat, colourist tradition was replaced by a linear modelling technique called *cunfa*, where depth and texture are defined in brush strokes rather than shading. This eventually gave way to an ink monochrome landscape tradition which was enthusiastically adopted by scholars and court painters alike, spawning a host of contending schools. In Japan, however, the poetic, colourist Tang style was retained and its emotive potential was developed so far that eventually *Yamato-e* painting had little in common with either its Chinese contemporary style or its Tang sources.

The culmination of japanization may be seen in the 1053 Byōdōin Phoenix Hall murals. *Yamato-e* landscape paintings were greatly influenced by the highly developed Japanese literature of the time, that is, poems on the four seasons, on famous scenic spots, on *mono-no-aware* (or the pathos, literally the 'ah-ness', of things). Departing from Chinese notions of Spring, for example, indigenous new poems replace the snow prunus with cherry blossoms, majestic mountains with cosy paddy fields. The world of Japanese imagery shimmered with wisteria, the seashore, spring rains, spring moon and spring mists, in poetry and painting alike.

57   An example is the *Early Spring Landscape* on a door panel of the Phoenix Hall. A gentle river scene combines lushness and a sense of intimacy typical of Japanese landscapes with favourite details: the meandering river, the sand shoal with its few reeds remaining from last year still covered in snow, the pine-clad hills and the thatched roofs of the cottages. The colours are applied in flat layers, with volume suggested by discreet intensification of the greens and whites. The only sense of motion is provided by the rippling lines of the river bend. The later predilection for laterally spreading motifs is hinted at here in the fan shaped silhouettes of the pines.

The simplicity of the scene belies the sophistication of its rendering. It is evocative and poetic. Perhaps it depicts one of the Famous Places so often mentioned in Heian literature, as do so many later so-called decorative screens. But if we were to consider such work as being merely decorative we would miss a good deal of the emotion peculiar to Japanese art. Decorative art is passive and static, with visual elements harmoniously interacting; this scene is vibrantly alive and invites an emotional response from the spectator. (See, for instance, the free-floating cloud forms, where the pigment is sprinkled on, rather than brushed. The clouds seem to breathe, and so seem charged with motion and emotion in the otherwise still space. They function as emotional indicators henceforth, providing this quickening and poignancy. We may call this unique motif the 'emotive cloud'.) The Heian artist may have chosen this scene, and this way of depicting it, in order to express the first quivering of New

57 *Early Spring Landscape.* Door panel in Phoenix Hall, Byōdōin. 1053.

Year's joys: he may even have been inspired by a poem in the contemporary anthology *Gosenshū* (951 AD):

mizu no omo ni	The breezes of spring
aya fukimidaru	Are blowing the ripples astray
haru kaze ya	Along the water . . .
ike no kōri wo	Today they will surely melt
kyō wa tokuramu	The sheet of ice on the pond.

(Ki no Tomonori, trans. Donald Keene)

The Heian preoccupation with minutely identified emotion found expression in poetry which led to painting, diaries, letters, screens and narrative handscrolls. Even in gardens of the period, both real and those shown in screen paintings, plants, shrubs, streams and stones were deliberately arranged to evoke specific emotions, or to recreate Famous Places which had poetic associations. A unique feature is the cloud-form island covered with white sand which appears in pond gardens and garden manuals of the time. The free-form 'emotive cloud', *kumogata*, seen

79

perhaps, as a reflection of the sky, evoked in sprinkled pigment on paper a subtle confirmation of the indefinable, the transient and the moving. In Heian art, nature motifs functioned to express human emotions. Not only did Heian architecture encourage maximum integration of interior space with garden, but the sliding door panels (*shōji*), which often surrounded three sides of a room, were themselves adorned with evocative landscapes.

But the dichotomy between the public and private sense persisted. Official, public architecture was termed *hare*. It had tiled roofs, slated floors and red lacquered pillars in the Chinese manner. The Emperor's private residence, however, was emphatically in the domestic mode termed *ke*, with thatched roof, wooden floors and pristine, unpainted pillars. In the first scroll of the *Ban Dainagon E-kotoba*, where Fujiwara no Yoshifusa is shown advising the Emperor, the double standard is apparent: in the outer vestibule the mural is in the public, Chinese style, while murals in *Yamato-e* style decorate his private rooms. In general, art for public places and ceremonial events used Chinese motifs. In the palace, the *Screen of Sages* shows Chinese sages, and the *Lake Kunming* screen has Chinese references. Because they were associated with the pomp of the Tang court or the much admired Confucian tradition, Chinese-style paintings carried great prestige. In time, such paintings came to be called *Kara-e* or Chinese (theme) painting, in contrast to *Yamato-e* or Japanese (theme) painting.

Handscroll painting

The *Yamato-e* painting of Japanese subject-matter developed some unique features in the illustrated narrative handscrolls, or *emaki-mono*, which were significantly an art practised by members of the court. Handscroll painting or calligraphy is an intimate format. The handscroll is unrolled (30 to 80 cm at a time) over a desk and perused at leisure: artist and spectator communicate one to one. Work for such a project was divided among a great number of painting masters (*eshi*, often members of the aristocracy), who selected the scenes, laid down the drawing for the compositions and indicated the colouring; artisans then mixed the pigments and filled in the colours.

Most celebrated of aristocratic artworks are the narrative handscrolls illustrating *The Tale of Genji*, a romance of Japanese court life written in the late tenth century by Lady Murasaki Shikibu. The earliest set of illustrations on this theme comes from 1120–30 and only survives in fragments: nineteen segments of illustrations and twenty of narrative in

59

58,64

58 Kashiwagi I (detail from *The Tale of Genji*). Handscroll; ink and colours on paper. Early 12th century.

elegant *kana* calligraphy by at least four great calligraphers of the day. (Today, these fragments are divided between the Tokugawa and Gotō museums.) The writing of the text is considered as important an art form as the paintings themselves.

The novel of fifty-four chapters originally must have covered at least twenty separate scrolls with hundreds of illustrations and thousands of sheets of calligraphy. The surviving illustrations are mostly from the last, so-called 'ten chapters of Uji', and our understanding of the style and techniques of the whole work is necessarily incomplete. Unlike didactic Buddhist illustrations, aimed at common folk, the Genji paintings and calligraphies are works of art that were circulated among aristocratic connoisseurs. It should be stressed that the paintings reveal a twelfth-century nostalgia and melancholy for the passing of the old Heian order of poetry and peace.

In the scene depicted in *Kashiwagi I*, the retired Emperor Suzaku, now a 58 monk, is full of concern for his daughter Princess Nyosan, and is quietly weeping. His daughter, stricken with guilt and remorse at having Kashiwagi's child, is insisting upon taking the tonsure. She is prostrate on the tatami on the left, unable to tell her father the truth or to face her husband Genji (seated below centre). Genji, for his part, is full of compassion for his wife and tries to dissuade her from her vows. In the text Genji is described as regretting his own inability to give up the worldly life, and envying his father-in-law's resolution. To the right, behind the curtains, ladies-in-waiting share in the sorrow.

Nowhere in this painting is there characterization or facial expression. The mask-like faces are painted in the technique known as *hikime kagihana* (line-eye hook-nose), which indicates features but does not identify individuals. (Reading the calligraphy portions, one would be familiar with the text, and would recognize the characters by their relative positions and postures.) Characteristically, such scenes show the tension just preceding an action, not the action itself. The ancient technique of *fukinuki yatai*, a bird's-eye view with the ceiling and often wall partitions removed, is used to great effect in the surviving Genji fragments, nearly all of which show indoor scenes.

This apparently tranquil scene, nevertheless, reveals emotional turbulence by subtle and effective means. The psychological isolation of the characters is symbolized by the silk room-dividers which are here placed to form cells of separate emotion. Elegant black ribbons hang from the curtains, in disarray, between the princess and her father and beside the ladies-in-waiting: this allows the artist to show strong emotion without giving his characters unseemly gesticulations. The tension is further heightened by the sharply tilted ground-plane.

64   In *Suzumushi II*, the painter has combined two episodes from the narrative. Genji has been unexpectedly invited by the Emperor Reizei, his supposed half-brother, for a moon-viewing party. Genji and his friends immediately set out for the palace, delighted that the spontaneous call shows a lessening of court formalities, at least on this occasion. In fact Reizei, here facing Genji, who is seated against the central pillar, has just renounced the throne upon discovering that Genji is not his half-brother but his actual father. In the text, flutes are played on Genji's way to the palace; but in the painting the artists have depicted an idyllic, moonlit flute concert on the Emperor's verandah.

In this painting, the tilt of the ground-plane is less steep than in *Kashiwagi I*, and the parallel lines formed by the balustrade, tatami mat borders and exposed beams provide a sense of relaxation and harmony. The meeting of Genji and his son is a poignant moment and both men are shown with heads inclined towards each other, prevented by stringent court etiquette from direct utterance of emotion. (Language, conduct and posture were so rigidly regulated in the eleventh and twelfth centuries that courtiers developed uncanny sensitivity to the slightest nuances of behaviour and situation. This allowed court paintings to depict scenes of pyschological intensity in compositions of apparent physical inertia.)

The articulate Lady Sei Shonagon, a contemporary of the author of *The Tale of Genji*, remarked that certain things suffer when depicted in paint, particularly some species of flowers and 'characters in fiction who have been praised for their beauty'. (Any attempt by the artist at interpretation of an idealized person or deity interferes with the spectator's own concept.) This widely held view accounts for the abstracted faces in the *Tale of Genji* scrolls, a convention also recognizable in Heian Buddhist painting and sculpture. However, the *hikime kagihana* technique allows the depiction of extremely subtle emotional nuances. In *Suzumushi II*, for example, the characters' eyebrows and eyes are built up from many fine, straight lines into thick layers, with the eyebrows high on the foreheads; the pupils of the eyes are single dots, exactly placed along the eyeline. Reizei's pupil is placed towards the centre of his face, to indicate warmth and humility; that of the figure on the extreme left, vivacity and gaiety.

The 'rule of taste' also developed colour consciousness to a high degree. The art of combining colours in daily wear revealed breeding as surely as tastes in poetry, calligraphy, incense and even paper for love letters, or as the way one conducted one's amorous affairs. The following passage from Lady Murasaki's diary (trans. Ivan Morris) makes this clear:

The Empress was wearing the usual scarlet robe, under which she had kimonos of light plum, light green and yellow rose. His Majesty's outer robe was made of grape-coloured brocade; underneath he had a willow-green kimono and, below that, one of pure white – all most unusual and up-to-date in both design and colour . . . Lady Nakazukasa's robe, which was also of grape-coloured brocade, hung loosely over a plain jacket of green and cherry.

On that day all the ladies in attendance on His Majesty had taken particular care with their dress. One of them, however, had made a small error in matching the colours at the openings of her sleeves. When she approached His Majesty to put something in order, the High Court Nobles and Senior Courtiers who were standing nearby noticed the mistake and stared at her. This was a source of lively regret to Lady Saishō and the others. It was not really such a serious lapse of taste; only the colour of one of her robes was a shade too pale at the opening.

It is a pity that the colours in paintings and scrolls have changed with time so that we are unable fully to appreciate the original tones and hues. The subtlety and refinement of colour-matching in Heian art is among the highest achievements of any ancient society. Even so, we can still easily see and respond to the strong sense of *mono-no-aware* which suffuses Heian perception of nature, people and art. It is an emotional shorthand, instantly leading from the perception of beauty to a melancholy consciousness of the transience of human life.

As was said above, there was in the Heian period an acute awareness of the distinction between public formality and private emotion. The public world was associated with the masculine (*otoko*) principle and seen in such public or *hare* manifestations as Chinese-style architecture and *kanshi* poetry in Chinese script. The inner world is expressed in the feminine (*onna*) mode, and with indigenous arts such as the Japanese syllabary script *kana* which perfectly suits polysyllabic Japanese poetry. Heian courtiers took pride in their command of Chinese *belles lettres*; but they also reserved native styles for their most intimate thoughts and feelings.

It is likely that this dichotomy caused the emergence of the terms *onna-e* feminine painting and *otoko-e* masculine painting in Heian writings. Some scholars have interpreted these terms as describing the gender of the subjects or of the artists or as referring to the style itself. But given the dramatic contrast between the exterior and interior worlds of Heian courtiers, it is possible to identify *onna-e* with introvert, emotional feeling and *otoko-e* with extrovert, physical action. (*Otoko-e* are often associated with historical events, such as the founding of monasteries, or wars where the focus is on actual events.) Each style of painting uses different techniques.

Onna-e (the style of the *Tale of Genji* scrolls) achieves pictorial stillness through subtle compositional devices such as those described earlier, and the style is equally effective with and without colour. For particularly sumptuous scenes, whether in *onna-e* or *otoko-e* style, a laborious colouring process known as *tsukuri-e* was often used: the underdrawing was covered up by applications of colours in thick, flat layers with little gradation, after which the outlines were redrawn in a delicate, unbroken line. The precise, complex designs on costumes and crests were painted by specialists, with attention paid to the women's hair and the lacquered headgear of the men. Architectural features, such as beam-lines, tatami mat borders, and curtains of state were ruled, enhancing the visual impact by manipulating the groundplane angle and the spectator's vantage-point. The calligraphic sections were inscribed in fully developed *hiragana* script; the paper was often dyed in many shades and decorated with tiny shapes, cut from gold foil, called *kirigane*. Other examples of *onna-e* painting, including many frontispieces of the gorgeous *Heike Nōgyō* described below, combined the *tsukuri-e* technique with *kirigane* decoration in lavish opulence. In the following Kamakura period the monochrome *hakubyō* style, which used only fine ink lines with tiny red lip-accents, came into use.

About fifty years later than the *Genji* scrolls, but clearly influenced by their style and techniques, are the *Heike Nōgyō* (the *Lotus Sutra* scrolls) commissioned by members of the Taira clan (Hei-ke in their Chinese reading.) By this time, Taira no Kiyomori controlled almost half of Japan by force: his power was matched only by his immense wealth. Among Fujiwara courtiers, the military were still stigmatized as uncouth and uncultured and it may have been to counter this reputation that the Taira warriors undertook this project of simultaneous conspicuous piety and extravagant expense. The ascendancy of the Taira clan in fact marked a cultural shift from a courtly aristocracy, such as that described in *The Tale of Genji*, to one of martial overlordship. Kiyomori's sutra offerings, begun about 1164, are both a nostalgic glance at the past and proof of a strong desire to beat the aristocracy at their own high-culture game.

The *Lotus Sutra*, which preached the salvation of both women and men, had long been a favourite with court ladies. Sutra copying often involved joint efforts on a single scroll, through the writing out of which the copyists established karmic relationship with one another; it could also be done by hiring specialists in sutra-style calligraphy and paper decoration. In the case of Taira no Kiyomori, a total of thirty-three scrolls (five more than the twenty-eight chapters of the *Lotus Sutra*), was commissioned for dedication to the principal deity of Itsukushima Shrine, the Kanzeon Bosatsu (Avalokiteśvara) of the Thirty-Three Manifestations. Each member of the clan undertook the preparation of a scroll and tried to outdo the others. The result was the most lavishly decorated sutra collection ever produced, as can be seen from the frontispiece to the twenty-third chapter. This states that women who receive the teaching of Yakuō Bosatsu (Bhaisajya rāja) and live by it, will be reborn on a lotus flower into the Blissful Amida Paradise. In the illustration, a court lady 65 leans against her black lacquered armrest, holding a sutra scroll decorated by a red sash, her hair in disarray, billowing over a garment of at least six layers, suggesting the *jūni hitoe* or twelve-layered court robe. Her youthful, pear-shaped face is turned towards golden shafts of light radiating from the aureole of the Welcoming Amida Raigō, descending on a purple cloud. The clouds are sprinkled with silver-white pigment; *kirigane* as well as pieces of silver foil of various sizes are liberally used. (They were applied individually, by rubbing a stiff brush through the hair to produce static electricity, then using the brush to pick up each foil piece and deposit it precisely. The metal dust was applied by flicking the brush, charged with gold or silver pigment, against one finger.)

Words from the sutra are camouflaged as part of the painting. The word 'born' is emerging at the top, as the new soul arrives, on the lotus pedestal. This techinique of hidden writing is called *ashide*, and was often used in *Yamato-e* painting, particularly in *onna-e*. If the frontispiece had been painted in the *otoko-e* tradition, the heavenward journey of the dying woman would have been physically shown, not symbolized in this way.

Otoko-e or masculine painting

The robust, action-filled narrative painting known as *otoko-e* is in complete contrast to the static and emotion-filled *onna-e*. Historical events are realistically depicted and uninhibited emotions are plainly shown in physical movement and facial expressions. Even the brush-strokes of landscape are charged with action; lines swell and shrink and large, dramatic and varied strokes are used simultaneously to create and to accent the pictorial composition.

A particularly accomplished group of three painted scrolls, known as the *Shigisan Engi*, depicts miracles performed by the devout ninth-century monk Myōren of Mount Shigi. (Scholars are puzzled by the lack of a prior, complete, source-text on which the narrative might have been based.) In the section shown, the painter depicts a miracle worked by the golden bowl Myōren used to send to be filled at the granary of a wealthy townsman. One day the servants left it in the granary, whereupon the magic bowl slipped out, dipped under the building and carried the entire store of rice back up the mountain. The townsfolk can be seen rushing after it, with wild gesticulations. The vantage-point is high (the only similarity with the *Tale of Genji* scrolls), and the narrative is continuous, the painting spreading over the entire scroll – a remarkable exploitation of the handscroll format. The second and third scrolls each have two sections, written narrative and painting. (One wonders whether the first scroll also had a calligraphic narrative, now lost.) The paintings date from between 1156, when the palace shown was rebuilt, and 1180, when it burned down. The anonymous artists would have been either *eshi* or imperial court painters familiar with obscure details of Buddhist incono-graphy, or else *ebusshi*, Buddhist painters based in Nara, with access to the imperial palace and with knowledge of court customs, a factor which makes even more striking the liveliness and veracity with which they depicted ordinary folk. This reflects a twelfth-century aristocratic interest in everyday matters, a characteristic of the new age.

Instead of heavy, opaque *tsukuri-e* style, the *Shigisan* scrolls show how the artists used colour transparently and sparingly to highlight the dynamic brushwork. Lively brushwork had been used since the Nara period for underdrawing, but now surfaces as 'legitimate' art in its own

66

right. Another illustration from the *Shigisan* scrolls, this time from Scroll III, can be seen on p. 51. It shows Myōren's sister, a nun, arriving at Tōdaiji, and uses six exposures to show consecutive actions, a characteristic of narrative painting. In this illustration, reading from right to left, the nun is seen praying to the Great Buddha, begging for a dream to lead her to her brother, the monk Myōren. She steps out to sleep and dreams she is inside again and is told to 'go toward the southwest and the mountain overhung with purple clouds'. She thanks the Buddha and is seen again, at daybreak, standing confidently on the steps of the Buddha Hall, facing the southwest ready to depart. In a sixth exposure, further left, she is on her way, beneath the great steps. The Great Buddha and its magnificent Hall are depicted in their original proportions before they are burnt down in the Taira war of 1180.

In the *Ban Dainagon E-kotoba* the lively brushwork of the *Shigisan* scrolls is combined with gorgeous colouring, which places the work stylistically somewhere between the courtly *onna-e Genji* scrolls and the lively *otoko-e Shigisan*. Although in *Ban Dainagon* some courtly interiors use thick *tsukuri-e* colouring, and some aristocratic features are abstractly depicted in the *hikime kagihana* manner, in general both facial expressions and gestures show clear emotions. *Genji* is a tale of social and emotional affairs, whereas *Ban Dainagon* is about political intrigue. It is a penetrating study of human motives and behaviour and is a valuable source of information about manners, and textile patterns, in the twelfth century.

The story is based on actual historical events of the ninth century. In 866 the evil minister Tomo no Yoshio (better known by his court rank Ban Dainagon) set fire to the main gate of the imperial palace and accused his rival Minamoto no Makoto of the deed. As Minamoto was about to be sentenced for the crime, the Prime Minister pleaded with the Emperor to suspend proceedings for lack of evidence. Several months elapsed. In the autumn of that year a quarrel broke out between the son of a butler in the metropolitan guard and the son of Ban Dainagon's accountant. The latter, presuming on the high rank of his employer, thrashed the butler's son, whereupon the outraged butler shouted that he knew the secret evil doings of Ban Dainagon. Gossip spread this observation and the butler was summoned to court for questioning. He said that he had personally seen Ban Dainagon and his son set fire to the Gate but had not dared to report the deed because of Ban Dainagon's power. Ban Dainagon was sentenced to banishment. The scrolls show both nobles and commoners, and vividly characterize both types.

In the illustration shown, multiple exposure technique (showing consecutive actions anti-clockwise) is used to depict the pivotal scene of

59

the children's quarrel. In the upper right, surrounded by curious townsfolk, the butler's son, wearing a short, blue robe with polka-dots, is having his hair pulled by the accountant's son. Next (upper centre) we see the accountant rushing to the rescue, fists at the ready. He shields his son (below left), who sneers triumphantly as his father kicks the butler's son, sending him staggering to the left. Then (upper left) we see the accountant's wife dragging her reluctant son home to be chastised. Again, architectural details give clues to the date and creator of the work. The accurate representation of the Kaishō-mon Gate, which was burnt down in 1177 and not rebuilt, gives the latest possible date for the scroll. As the Seiryōden Imperial Residence is inaccurately drawn, we may assume either that the artist did not have access to the innermost recesses of the Palace or that the place shown was a temporary residence of the Emperor. On the other hand, the artist has represented the metropolitan police force with an impressive and rigorous accuracy which suggests intimate familiarity with that agency.

A unique and splendid set of scrolls in the ink monochrome *hakubyō* tradition and in the *otoko-e* manner has also survived from the period. The four scrolls are collectively known as *Chōjū Giga* (Frolicking Animals). The first two can be dated definitely from the first half of the twelfth century, while the third and fourth scrolls, of lesser quality in brushwork and slightly different in content, date from the mid-thirteenth. The *Chōjū Giga* scrolls have no accompanying, or even a separate, text; they are the work of Buddhist monks and their often hilarious content has been the subject of much remark. The first scroll shows human games, rituals and other activities performed by animals often dressed as humans. The second scroll shows some fifteen kinds of real or fantasy animals. The third scroll shows monks and laymen at play, then animals parodying their actions. The fourth (notably inferior) scroll continues the satirical theme.

This gentle clerical caricature reveals humorous and compassionate observation of human foibles during the moral decay of the twelfth century. In the example from the first scroll, a monkey dressed as a monk is offering a peach branch before the Buddhist altar; his ceaseless chant is shown by wavy ink lines coming from his mouth. The simian offering is solemnly accepted by a corpulent frog, proudly seated on a lotus leaf, with a giant banana leaf as his aureole. He is framed by leafless branches of a gnarled tree, drawn in a few swelling ink strokes. Beyond the horizon, late autumnal grasses sway in the wind as three clerics (two foxes and a monkey) show various states of mortification and *ennui*. Nearby, a fox and a hare, clutching Buddhist rosaries, are also uttering incantations.

60

59 *Ban Dainagon E-kotoba*: the children's quarrel. Handscroll; second of three scrolls; ink and colours on paper. Late 12th century.

60 Simian prelate worshipping frog Buddha, from *Chōjū Giga* scrolls. Ink on paper. Late 12th century.

Elsewhere in the scroll there are scenes of animals wrestling, riding, picnicking and taking part in archery contests and water sports. Whether or not they refer directly to the annual court festivals and sports, such as those listed in the *Nenjū gyōji*, cannot be proven, but there is no mistaking the whimsical caricature of humanity. The art of ink caricature was revived in the mid-Edo period of the eighteenth and nineteenth centuries, when cartoons, *manga*, became a favoured genre and launched great artists such as Katsushika Hokusai.

It would be pointless to discuss Japanese narrative painting solely in terms of Chinese origins. Certainly, various Chinese narrative scrolls had been seen by Japanese in China and, occasionally, in Heian collections. The two Japanese linear traditions, the discreet, unwavering 'iron-wire' line seen in *onna-e* and the oblique swelling and diminishing line of *otoko-e* painting, were both basic to Chinese figurative painting. But the Chinese used figurative representation to exemplify general moral precepts, and descriptions of specific events or physical traits served to represent the universal values of a moral society where the arts were expected to inspire the beholder. The Japanese artist, by contrast, guided only by courtly standards of taste, was free to explore the smallest detail of the human condition. It was not considered improper to express personal feelings; in fact, such expression was encouraged and the remarkable acuity of observation so developed led to some of the most masterly narrative paintings the world has seen.

Continuation of narrative scroll traditions

Illustrated narrative handscrolls grew in popularity in the Kamakura period. They had been the oldest means for Buddhist proselytizing among the masses since Tang Chinese story-tellers held up painted scenes to illustrate their market-place narratives.

Japanese religious education continued the practice. *Ebusshi* illustrated not only the glories of Paradise but the frightful torments of Hell. This type of didactic Buddhist painting is known as *rokudō-e* (Painting of the Six Paths) and its subject matter was drawn from the six regions of the Impure Land in contrast to the elysian Pure Land. Its purpose was to warn those who did not ceaselessly recite Amida's name that they were risking disease, deformity and all the horrors of Hell. *Hungry Ghosts*, for example, now in the Tokyo National Museum, graphically shows how attachment to worldly things in this life leads to similar bondage in the next. After death, former gluttons experience hunger pangs. Here they are seen feasting on the fecal matter of unwary slum dwellers. The

61

61 *Hungry Ghosts*, from the *Gaki Zōshi* scroll (Kawamoto version). Ink, colours on paper. Late 12th century.

accurately perceived bloated abdomens and the frightening expressions on the ghostly faces were intended to teach medieval gluttons the Buddhist dictum, 'Leave the table when six-tenths full!'

Myōe in meditation

In 1206, the monastic reformer Kōben (a.k.a. Myōe-Shōnin, 1173–1232) re-established the forested mountain retreat Kōzanji, southwest of Kyoto, as an active part of the Kegon School of Buddhism of which Tōdaiji in Nara was the centre. Kōzanji became known for its remarkable paintings. Myōe is said to have imported many Chinese Song paintings and they may have influenced the new Kōzanji painting style. The first were produced by Myōe's favourite disciple, Enichi-bō Jōnin. His famous and unusual portrait of Myōe is a lasting tribute to the affection between the painter and his subject. It also introduces a new freshness and clarity in coloration. The abbot, in deep meditation, is portrayed three-quarter face, sitting in a tree. His eyes are closed, his smile-wrinkles are emphasized and his resolute, shaven but bristly chin is depicted with striking realism. This outstanding portrait signals the new spiritual vigour of the Kamakura period, when aristocratic and aesthetic indulgence began to give way to a new sense of moral purpose and dynamism.

62

After a long period of diplomatic isolation, Japan was now welcoming Chinese works showing the new Song spirit of spartan introspection, a contrast to the previous opulent extravagance of Tang. This reflects a shift of power in China from the courtly aristocracy to a scholarly bureaucracy. In art, inner spiritual qualities were stressed rather than external details. Transparent colour-washes were preferred to heavy pigmentation. The development of modelling strokes replaced colour shading.

The portrait of Myōe is a Japanese interpretation of these new Song ideas. The brushwork is firm but supple; the forms express inner tranquillity; the rocks are built up by parallel contour lines with occasional dark accents; finely sketched tree outlines are superimposed by lines of broader wash.

The *engi* (founding history) of the Kegon School was produced at Kōzanji at Myōe's request. The six illustrated scrolls of the *Kegon Engi* are widely considered to have been painted by Enichi-bō Jōnin. The Korean patriarchs of the School, Gishō and Gengyō (Korean: I-sang and Won-hyo), who introduced Kegon (Korean: Hwa-on) teachings from Silla in the seventh century, are the subjects of the narrative. The first four scrolls are devoted to Gishō (624–702), who studied Buddhism in China and was there adored by a beauty named Zemmyō (Chinese: Shanmiao), whom he converted to the Buddhist faith. As Gishō's boat was about to sail for Korea, Zemmyō threw her parting gift after it. To her surprise the gift began to follow the boat as if alive; this inspired Zemmyō to plunge into the ocean herself, whereupon she was transformed into a large dragon and carried Gishō's boat on her back to Korea. (Zemmyō thereafter was deified as patron goddess of the Kegon School.)

67 In the detail shown, her transformation has been accepted by the passengers who are listening as Gishō, in the centre, expounds the Law. As in the Myōe portrait, the painting is relaxed, the brushwork is clear and supple and although every space is full there is no sense of crowding. On the contrary, the soft colour gradations, as the sea turns from blue to white, give a sense of spaciousness. There is none of the drama found in the assertive brushwork of *Shigisan Engi*, and none of the emotional intensity of the *Genji* scrolls. Instead there is a sparkling clarity, reflecting the shift in emphasis from emotion to spirituality.

War tales

A later, major category of picture handscrolls tells of heroism and loyalty in battle. The illustrations are based on literary tales or historical chronicles of specific engagements. This development marks the start of

62 *Myōe Shōnin* meditating, by Enichi-bō Jōnin. Hanging scroll; ink, colours on paper. Early 13th century.

military overlordship in Japan, where the *bakufu* form of government began in 1185 with Minamoto Yoritomo's seizure of power and the establishment of his government in Kamakura. From then to the end of Tokugawa rule in 1868, interest in the code of the warrior (*bushidō*) was reflected in the vast production of war tales, both in literature and in all kinds of fine art: fan painting, album leaves, screens and hanging scrolls as well as narrative handscrolls.

Like a film, the handscroll depicts action in sequence, one frame at a time. The pace at which the narrative takes the viewer's attention is intentionally directed. Each scroll painting has its own tempo, fast or slow, which engages the viewer to the extent of conditioning the speed at which he unrolls the scroll. In the *Genji* scroll, for instance, the pictorial sections are separate paintings interleaved with a continuous calligraphic narrative. This 'internal', *onna-e*, style makes the viewer pause at length over each 'frame' to savour every detail of its meaning, whereas the *otoko-e* style of many war scrolls is more explicit, with continuous action scenes and no textual interruption. The tales of *Shigisan Engi* and *Ban Dainagon e-kotoba* and the *Kegon Engi* are examples of this type. With the growing interest in battle techniques, the detailed depiction of each stage in combat became a crucial feature of handscroll painting. The urgency of tactical manoeuvres brings to the combat narratives a dramatic new dimension.

94

63 Burning of the Sanjō palace in Kyoto by the rebel Minamoto forces. Detail from *Heiji monogatari* scrolls. Ink, colours on paper. Late 13th century.

An early, important set of scrolls, the *Heiji monogatari*, describes the crucial battle of 1159 in the civil war between the Minamoto (Genji) and Taira (Heike) clans. The scrolls are based on a novel of the same name written in 1220. Another novel, about a similar conflict in the Hōgen era (1156), called the *Hōgen monogatari*, was written in the same year. Both of these use a new, plain-spoken language where the battle scenes are described in a direct and epic manner. Three scrolls from at least fifteen describing the Heiji wars have survived.

The illustration shows the burning of the Imperial Palace at Sanjō in   63
Kyoto, as the rebel (Minamoto) forces try to seize power by capturing the Emperor. The instigator of the revolt was Fujiwara Nobuyori, who had conspired with Minamoto no Yoshitomo. The *coup* was staged in December of 1159 and the retired Emperor Go-Shirakawa taken prisoner. The section illustrated shows the Imperial Palace in flames, while Minamoto forces the Emperor to board the cart waiting to take him to captivity. Other soldiers are shown charging on horseback, beheading imperial guards and spearing royal retainers; ladies weep helplessly or flee.

The scene is packed with multiple actions some of which are simultaneous, some sequential. It is a far more complex conception than the crowd scenes in *Ban Dainagon* or *Shigisan Engi*, where focus tended to be on a single action. The pace is more urgent and the action moves purposefully from right to left, in spite of vignettes (like film 'freeze frames'), which face right. The figures are grouped in triangles or in lozenges which culminate in a point; single figures lead from each group to the next. This spatial organization allows swift visual comprehension and thus quickens the pace. Unlike the caricatures of twelfth-century scrolls which often resort to exaggeration and caricature, thirteenth-century narratives stress physical realism. Like its literature, Kamakura painting was action-packed and spirited, dealing with real moments, with no allusions to other times or themes. The fire, for example, is seen in several time-lapses, from its explosive outburst to the tongues of flame licking the adjoining roofs and then to the smoke-filled, red clouds rising heavenwards, bringing a fall-out of burning cinders. (These last were made by flicking a paint-charged brush across the wrist, covering the paper with red dots.) At the centre of the fire the heat is most intense and the flames are painted sharp and straight, devouring the charred beams. Patronage has changed from the courtly Fujiwara to the martial Minamoto, and the arts sensitively reflect the shift in aesthetics.

Kana calligraphy: onnade

The Japanese regard the development and perfection of their indigenous calligraphy style as the quintessence of the Heian contribution to art. This achievement is all the more remarkable because of the unbridgeable differences between Chinese and Japanese speech, poetry and attitudes towards written script. Between the ninth and eleventh centuries an ingenious system of adapting Chinese characters was evolved, and in the hands of courtiers developed into an expression of the highest order.

Since prehistoric times, the Chinese had shown a need and respect for the art of writing. Ideographic units, either pictographs or ideographs, evolved, each representing a specific idea. They are monosyllabic and were first used only by diviner-scribes of the priestly shaman kings such as the Shang kings (fourteenth century BC) to communicate with ancestral spirits. Later, the deeds of Zhou nobles were recorded and writing was widely adopted as a means of recording such things as military orders, history and poetry. Chinese verse uses couplets or quatrains of four, five or seven syllables; symmetry is bilateral: that is, nouns, verbs or adjectives, contrasting or paired, appear in comparable positions in the

64 Suzumushi II, detail from *The Tale of Genji* scrolls. Ink, colours on paper. Early 12th century. (See p. 82)

65 Yakuō Bosatsu Honjibon, detail from *Heike Nōgyō* handscrolls. Ink, colours on paper, with kirigane decoration. *c.* 1164. (See p. 85)

respective phrases and thus, when inscribed, occur side by side in vertical columns, written from top to bottom and ranging from right to left. By the time Chinese script appeared in Japan in the fifth century AD, by way of Korea, it was twenty centuries old and standardized.

The Japanese, on the other hand, throughout their millennia of ceramic history, had been content with an oral transmission of poetry and legends in songs and dances. The need for written documents was felt only with the advent of a centralized government and its diplomacy. In the fifth century, Chinese books on Confucian classics, the histories and literary selections began to enter Japan and from the sixth century onwards, Buddhist sutras, written in Chinese, also became known. In the late sixth century, Prince Shōtoku had the articles of state of his newly constructed government written down in Chinese, which was learned by the ruling classes. China had come to be regarded as the source of all civilization.

Chinese is linguistically alien to the Japanese speaker and its mastery by an adult required then, as it does now, prodigious effort. To use the Chinese writing system to transcribe the Japanese language was an even more formidable task. Chinese is monosyllabic and non-inflected while Altaic-Tungusic Japanese is polysyllabic and agglutinative with a great variety of suffixes for verbs and adjectives. In the first written history of Japan, Chinese syntax prevailed. In the histories compiled in 712 and 720, Japanese names were transcribed syllable for syllable, using Chinese characters of approximately equivalent sound value, just as the Chinese themselves had once transcribed the Indian names of Buddhist deities. But whereas the Chinese remained faithful to their original transcription of Sanskrit or other alien sounds, the Japanese delighted in the myriad visual puns made possible by substituting one of several (visual) Chinese characters for the same (aural) syllable. At first they resolutely refused to relate the fifty-one syllable sounds of the Japanese language to fifty-one standard Chinese characters.

This method of transcription was based on what has come to be called the *on-yomi* or phonographic system of sound value. Here the Chinese pictograph for fish would be read *wu* (the contemporary reading along the South China coast) and was used as a phonetic element of a polysyllabic word. The ideographic system was called *kun-yomi*, and here the pictograph for fish would be given its Japanese sound value, *sakana*, and would mean fish. Early Japanese writing used both systems, as seen in the first poetry anthology, the *Manyōshū*, which contains 4,500 poems written prior to 760 AD. But due to the complex and deliberately irregular method of transcription, some of the poems remain unsolved textual puzzles to this day.

From the ninth century, Japanese writers began to replace this cumbersome method with a syllabic system in which various preferred Chinese characters were reduced to a few strokes each and read only for sound values. Its angular *katakana* form was derived from the formal Chinese *kaishu* script and was used in Japan for official documents, Buddhist sutras and printing; its cursive, *hiragana* form, came from the informal Chinese draft script, *caoshu*. This was a tremendous step forward. The Japanese language with its polysyllabic cadences and long vowel stresses, so conducive to recitation and singing, was at last provided with a written equivalent based on sounds and not concepts.

The *katakana* syllabary was used for phonetic glosses to Chinese texts and for Japanese written in the Chinese *kun* system but needing suffixes, while the *hiragana* system was developed for use in transcribing Japanese poetry (*waka*), for the writing of personal letters and for new literary forms such as romances and diaries. Men thought it was unbecoming for women to struggle with Chinese learning and it became a tacit social taboo for women to be seen holding a book in Chinese. Thus men engaged in Chinese studies and used Chinese script for their Chinese and Japanese poetry, whereas women wrote only in Japanese. Their *hiragana* style of calligraphy came to be called *onnade* (feminine hand). By the late eleventh century, as Fujiwara culture was reaching its peak, *onnade* achieved unsurpassed internal balance and grace. The example shown 68 here is the so-called *masu-shikishi* calligraphy, and recalls the pristine purity of the sculpture and murals of the Phoenix Hall. There is no trace of Chinese origin or of the extravagant flourishes to come. The writing was inscribed with a finely pointed brush usually held upright. The diagonal swings do not detract attention from a steady vertical axis which is never actually touched. Balance and dynamic energy are maintained in elements of different sizes, in the contrast between light and dark, in column alignment and in the density and openness of the internal spirals. Furthermore, the work shows creative originality and expressiveness which are never allowed to interfere with legibility.

The thirty-one syllable poem by Kiyohara no Fukayabu is transcribed below, line by line, as it appears in the calligraphy:

natsu no yo wa mada yoi na-	summer night still dusky and
gara akenuru wo kumo	yet day breaks: oh! clouds
no izukoni	somewhere among them
tsuki kakuru	the moon is hiding
ra-n	perhaps

The thin night air of summer is expressed in the fine lines of the first column. The artist breaks the word *nagara* (and yet) to gain power and momentum in the second column, where his brush tip is freshly charged with more ink and applied with firmer pressure. The letters *a-ke-nu* of the word *akenuru* (daybreak) literally expand, breaking apart, the *ke* occupying about four times the width of the preceding *nagara*. 'Daybreak' thus actually overlaps the *no izuko* (somewhere) of the next column, recreating the clouds which cover the moon at dawn.

This poem demonstrates simultaneous confidence in verbal and visual imagery. Not only are the phonetic elements, the *kana*, in a non-uniform size, but the inscription does not even conform to the internal metre of the

66 (*opposite above*) *The Flying Granary* (detail) from *Shigisan Engi*, first scroll. 1156–1180. (See p. 86)

67 (*below*) Zemmyō transformed into a dragon, detail from *Kegon Engi* handscrolls by Enichi-bō Jōnin. Early 13th century.

poem. An oral recitation of it would produce the following linear arrangement:

natsu no yo wa	summer night
mada yoi nagara	still dusky but already
akenuru wo	dawn breaks. Oh!
kumono izukoni	somewhere amidst the clouds
tsuki kakuru ra-n	surely the moon hides

However, the calligrapher has treated his task in visual, not aural terms. This freedom from extraneous considerations is an essentially Japanese quality. In Chinese calligraphy, the column length, once established, must be maintained. If a Chinese poet had written out the above poem in Japanese *kana* script, he would have either used lines of equal length and broken the metre or he would have reproduced the recitation pattern shown above. The Japanese poet has broken the lines for visual effect. The V-shaped silhouette with serrated edges represents the clouds parting, with the short, lowest (third) column emerging in a moon-like circle.

This poem was one of a pair written in an album format and later mounted separately on cards (*shikishi*). Such creative inscriptions of poetry took various forms. These included *tsugi-shikishi* where two contrasting sheets of paper provided the background for two poems and large or small *shikishi*, boards mounted with plain or decorated paper, which by the early twelfth century had to rival *tsukuri-e* painting itself in sumptuousness, as may be seen in the narrative sections of the *Genji* scrolls.

Eleventh century calligraphy paper was usually white or light blue; sutras, exceptionally, were done in Chinese block script, in gold paste on an indigo ground. Japanese paper designs, for poetry or prose, became ever more complicated. The material could be dyed before manufacture; the paper itself could be dyed or painted with colour and then sprinkled with cloudy, misty shapes. Other methods involved the imprinting of ink figures, gold or silver patterns, *kirigane* metal flakes, hair-fine metal slivers (*noge*) and metal dust (*sunago*). Colours included various hues of red, violet, indigo, blue, white, yellow, brown and green. Heian paper often imitated Chinese Tang and Song patterns and used the same woodblock printing techniques.

The high, bird's-eye-view perspective of vast expanses with low-lying hillocks and meandering streams, often associated with Heian landscape painting and paper decoration, had been long considered a Japanese contribution. However, Egami Yasushi has recently pointed out that such perspective is rare in Japanese works prior to the importation in 1073 of a set of Buddhist commentaries written out by the Chinese Emperor Song Taizong (he reigned 976–997) and illustrated by fifty Northern Song artists, and then made into woodblock printed editions. The imported book is a Korean copy but faithfully preserves the Song perspective and marked diagonality. While these characteristics were abandoned in China in succeeding ages, they took root in Heian Japan and contributed features to the *Yamato-e* tradition which persevere to this day.

Chinese motifs on calligraphy paper included the so-called 'Chinese grasses', bamboos, sparrows and lions, but Japanese motifs soon appeared, many of which are still favoured today. They include rabbits in autumn grasses, deer, flowing water (a motif traceable to Yayoi times), cherry blossoms, peaches, wild chrysanthemum and waves. Collage, where sheets torn or cut on the diagonal formed colourful designs, also became fashionable. Some papers were further decorated by painting: this provided underdrawing for the calligraphy.

Almost all Heian secular arts, picture scrolls, screens or lacquer decoration and fan paintings contain direct or indirect literary references. Calligraphy is naturally the most literature-based form of all. The *Sanjūrokunin ka shū* (Anthology of the Thirty-Six Poets) was produced in the early twelfth century and marks the highest achievement in the crafts of paper making and decoration. It is thought that this collection of hundreds of poems, inscribed by twenty calligraphers, was intended as a tribute to the retired Emperor Shirakawa on his sixtieth birthday in 1112. The following example is by Minamoto no Shigeyuki (died 1000):

> *eda wakanu*
> *haru ni a(h)edomo*
> *mumore*
> *gi wa*
> *Moemo masarade*
> *toshi he-*
> *nuruka-*
> *na*

Although the buried log encounters Spring, when branches emerge undivided How many years has it passed without greening!

The poem may refer to a mature woman, symbolized by the buried log, who has seen yet another spring come and go, bringing a loveless summer. It is painted in mica and ink upon collage-decorated paper. In the centre, an abandoned boat (a standard summer subject) is half hidden by reeds. It is painted on a torn fragment of paper inserted between two lighter coloured pieces, as if it were not of the same world. Above turbulent mica waves, tiny ink birds scatter and a small boat carrying two figures heads toward a minuscule island. The calligraphic alignment of the

68 (*left*) *Onnade* calligraphy from one of the *Masu-shikushi* set of calligraphies. *Shikishi* album leaf. Late 11th century. (See p. 99)

69 (*above*) Calligraphy fragment from the *Shigeyukishū* collection from the *Sanjūrokunin ka shū. c.* 1112.

poem follows the speech cadences, and complex Chinese characters are used to end the piece with a firm masculine flourish. In weighted and measured wrist pressure the calligrapher seems to have inscribed the secret agonies of the *waka* poem as if writing an official edict.

The calligraphy here differs in several respects from that of the previous example. It is not in the *onnade* or *hiragana* form of phonetic symbols, but in the more Chinese-oriented *sōgana* form, where syllables are mostly made of cursive forms of fuller Chinese characters. Secondly, the calligrapher pressed down more on his brush and slanted it from time to time to change the width of the strokes. There is no longer the continuity and flow of the late eleventh century nor the internal balance. The writing reveals self-conscious linkages between words and tight turns around the loops. The calligraphy occupies slightly more than half the double album-leaf format, with the literary source written out completely in Chinese in the last column. However, the Chinese characters are written with the same flowing quality and emphasis on lateral movement along the writing surface as Japanese Kana syllabary. The extensive decoration of the paper restricts the calligrapher's freedom in applying his script. There is a link with the heightened, indirectly expressed emotion of *onna-e* painting. At first glance, the calligraphy is stately and calm but the agitation betrayed in the second line, *haru ni aedomo* (though encountering Spring), shows that it is not a straightforward summer boating song but is resonant with

70 *Flowing Stream* with small birds. *Maki-e* on *koto*. 12th century.

unfulfilled emotions. The harsh breaks within *eda – wa – kanu* in the first column and in *haru – ni – a(h)edomo* in the second are stark and sudden like peals of thunder on a rainless summer day.

Lacquers

A remarkable development in both the technique and design of lacquer making is seen toward the latter part of the Heian period. Although scholars have not been able to reach a final conclusion on the origins of the technique (*maki-e*), where colour, gold and silver dust or particles are sprinkled onto still tacky lacquer, its use during the Fujiwara period shows that it was indisputably wedded to Japanese taste. The subtle shading of the dust creates nuances previously unseen in lacquers. In the earliest form of the process only the design is lacquered (*hira-makie*). In the later and more complex form, relief motifs (*taka-makie*), the entire surface of the utensil was covered with several applications of lacquer and colour or metal dust. Each lacquer layer was carefully sanded to even the surface and bring out the lustre, with main motifs rising above the surface. Mother-of-pearl inlay (*raden*) was also widely used.

In decoration, relatively crowded, evenly spread Tang Chinese motifs gave way to a new taste for asymmetrical arrangements and an increased use of empty space. Whether these tendencies can all be traced to Song designs remains to be studied, but their integration with the form of the utensil is as purely Japanese as the calligraphy described above. In one of the most beautiful examples of *maki-e* designs, gold and silver is finely wrought in the manner of late Heian decoration. In a later example from the Kamakura period, hidden writing (*ashide*), a popular practice, is camouflaged in silver low-relief on the rocks, bank and tree trunk. The design is vigorous and the techniques are more complicated.

70

105

CHAPTER FIVE

Kamakura and Muromachi (1185–1573)

By the mid-twelfth century rivalry between the Taira and Minamoto clans erupted in open warfare. Epic battles were fought in 1156 and 1160 and the land was devastated by famine and plague until the final triumph of Minamoto no Yoritomo at the tragic sea-battle of Dannoura in 1185. From then until the restoration of imperial control in 1868, a succession of military dictators governed Japan in the Emperor's name.

This military culture was unlike anything Japan or China had ever produced. It was founded on fidelity and honour for which one was always ready to die a violent death. Unlike the ceremonial swords of Heian courtiers which were usually sheathed, and in delicately crafted scabbards, the new, warrior's sword was a lethal blade of unsurpassed lightness and strength. Made of two layers of iron and steel which were subjected to repeated folding and beating, then to fire and immersion in water, Japanese *samurai* blades were marked by a unique vapour imprint called *ni-e*, much prized by connoisseurs.

The warrior developed a close relationship with Shintō shrines, like that of Heian aristocrats with Buddhist temples. The swordsmith's work thus took on a sacred aspect with extended rites of purification and abstinence before each new blade was forged. The swordsmith also wore pure white garments, an echo of the white vestments of the Shintō priest. Each sword was thought to take on its own spiritual life; success or failure in battle was attributed to the spirit in the sword.

Gifts of stunning workmanship were made to Shintō shrines, beginning with the Taira clan's donation of the *Lotus Sutra* scrolls and of the armour of Taira no Shigemori, Kiyomori's son. Each military commander identified himself with a particular shrine where he prayed for victory and offered thanks after battle. Thus, the Minamoto clan in Kamakura had links with the Tsurugaoka Shrine where Yoritomo made numerous gifts. His wife Masako patronized the shrine at Mishima and there offered up her exquisite lacquer toiletry box. The early thirteenth century sword called Masatsune was used for warfare until the early eighteenth century when the Shōgun Tokugawa Yoshimune made it a votive offering.

71

71 Armour with blue yarns from Taira clan. 12th century.

Military overlordship: the Shōgun and his bakufu

When Minamoto no Yoritomo seized political control in 1185, he moved the seat of power from Kyoto to the rugged eastern sea-coast of Kamakura. He instituted the *bakufu* form of government which ruled in the name of the nominally revered Emperor. Yoritomo's military government ruled with spartan resolution and vigour until 1333, demanding unquestioning obedience and rigorous discipline. In 1192 the Emperor confirmed Yoritomo's authority with the title of Barbarian-Subduing Supreme General – Shōgun. The Minamoto family continued in this position until their line died out when their regents, the Hōjō, took effective control. Government administration was in their hands, and the Shōgun himself (no longer of the Minamoto clan) became a puppet like the Emperor. None the less, fierce loyalty to the 'Lord of Kamakura' lived on in generations of faithful vassal families and maintained the integrity of the *bakufu:* even after the Mongol invasions of 1274 and 1281 when finances were low and internal corruption had loosened the *bakufu's* control, when loyalist supporters of Emperor Go-Daigo (1288–1339) twice attempted revolt, they only succeeded in obtaining the Emperor's banishment to Oki. In 1333, after the Kemmu Restoration, rival warrior clans supported different pretenders to the throne, creating a northern court in Kyoto and a southern court in Yoshino. The schism lasted for fifty-seven years until the southern Emperor Go-Kameyama abdicated in favour of Emperor Go-Komatsu (1377–1433). In 1392 the country was once more unified.

Kamakura sculpture

While the major arts, perfected during the Heian period, continued to flourish under martial rule, the new structure of society created new artistic demands. The great Tōdaiji and Kōfukuji monasteries of Nara which had supported Yoritomo's cause had, in consequence, been destroyed by Taira forces in 1180. Their reconstruction now began. In 1183 the Chinese sculptor Chen Hoqing was brought to Nara to recast the head of the Great Buddha of Tōdaiji but most of the restoration work was undertaken by Japanese artists, particularly those of the illustrious Kei school, descended from Jōchō of the Byōdōin sculptures. Jōchō's sons had established branches in Kyoto and Nara; it was one of the Nara descendants, Unkei (died 1223) who most strongly influenced Kamakura sculpture.

The restoration project at Tōdaiji, which lasted for several generations, involved close study of the Tang models and Tang-inspired works for repairs to the sculptures. This study, combined with the new, stimulating contact with Chinese Song models, led to heightened realism and simplicity; colouring became more subdued and new, emphatically human iconological types appeared. The spirit of reform in Buddhism, with its mass appeal, has already been noted in connection with the Kōzanji paintings.

Early works of the Unkei school are the last highpoint in Japanese sculptural history. At first sight, these sculptures appear to revive the eighth-century Nara style of realism; but whereas that was idealized, generic and impersonal, Kamakura realism involved both the depiction of physical characteristics and a clear feeling of each subject's particular spiritual likeness; dark-centred crystals were now first used to give life to the eyes.

Minamoto no Yoritomo was anxious to distance himself from debilitating court life, wishing to establish an image of virile, martial simplicity which would stress inner spiritual alertness rather than exterior grace. He wanted his own Pure Land Paradise enshrined in Kamakura – but not in the effete beauty of the late Fujiwara style. He consulted with Seichō, Unkei's uncle, then leader of the Nara sculptors, and with Tamehisa, a painter working in the new Song brush manner like that of Enichi-bō Jōnin. Unfortunately, the repository for this new art is no longer extant; but we know that Unkei was in eastern Japan, either as Seichō's assistant or on his own, during its construction.

A group of massive and compelling Buddhist images, some of Unkei's early works, are now to be found in the Ganjōjū-in in Shizuoka Prefecture. In 1752 an inscription was found inside one of them, stating that Unkei began work on the project in 1186, sponsored by Hōjō no Tokimasa, Yoritomo's father-in-law. It is likely that Unkei's years in the invigorating atmosphere of Kamakura contributed to the extraordinary vitality and intensity of his later works.

These works herald the birth of true Japanese portraiture. There is little doubt that Unkei was influenced by Song sculpture. Dry lacquer and pottery works produced in the eastern Chinese Liao-Jin dynasties between the tenth and thirteenth centuries show life-like people with distinct personalities. This reflects an interest in capturing inner essence through faithful outer modelling. None of this was lost on the young Unkei. His father, Kōkei, assumed leadership of the Nara school when Seichō died and Unkei returned to Nara to work on the Tōdaiji and Kōfukuji projects.

Muchaku portrays the Indian patriarch Asanga in carved painted wood, 72 and represents both Unkei's mature style and the best in Kamakura sculpture. The holy man stands life-size, his weight on the left foot, turning an intellectual and kind face slightly to the right. Unkei does not carve an idealized representation but portrays a real individual, probably the likeness of a particular Japanese Buddhist master known to him. Muchaku is one of the principal figures in Kōfukuji's North Octagonal Hokuendō Hall, and was sculpted between 1208 and 1212. Compared to non-iconic figures of the Nara period, such as the beautiful dry lacquer standing

73 figure of *Furuna* in the Kōfukuji which had doubtless impressed Unkei with its expressive force, Muchaku shows a fuller understanding of form and *contraposto* style. The sculptured figure is not poised as if about to fly, like the eighth-century figure: it stands balanced and relaxed. Song realism has here been heightened by the spiritual tautness peculiar to early Kamakura.

The work of Unkei's six sons and other disciples combined Song influences and indigenous developments in a similar way. These include the deep-cut and fluttering drapery in soft curves, more realistic hand and figure positions, pronounced but not exaggerated musculature, crystal eyeballs with darker pupils set in the sockets and, above all, spiritual intensity. These characteristics, however, are only hinted at in the principal icons: the further Buddhist iconography moved from India, the more rigid and conservative it became, allowing little artistic individuality.

The eldest of Unkei's six sculptor sons, Tankei (?1173–1256) was among his most remarkable followers. In the Rengeō-in, popularly known as the Hall of the Thirty-Three Bays (Sanjūsangendō) in Kyoto, Tankei and other Kei School masters left a seated senjū (thousand-armed) Kannon and a thousand smaller standing thousand-armed Kannons, all worked in bright gilt. Among images of the twenty-eight lay followers of this Kannon, two works by Tankei especially reflect the ardour and

74 intensity of Kamakura popular Buddhism. *Basū-sen* is shown as an old hermit of frail body but powerful features. Gaunt and bearded, he leans on a staff. As he stoops forward his right shoulder-bone protrudes; he holds a sutra scroll in his raised hand. The wrinkled face and swollen finger-joints show his age and deteriorated physical condition, but faith, piety and benevolence transform the lined face, with its sunken eyes and long curved nose, into a thing of beauty. Perhaps most compelling in its

75 simplicity and single-minded faith is a companion piece, *Mawara-nyō*, who stands erect with folded hands. Her neck muscles are taut; her mouth is firmly closed; her large eyes are wide and unblinking; her thoughts are focussed on inner spiritual realities, oblivious of passers-by. There is little here of such Heian qualities as *mono no aware*. Kamakura was not a time to

72 *Muchaku*, by Unkei. H. 188 cm. Kamakura, 1208–12.

73 *Furuna* (one of Ten Great Disciples). Painted dry lacquer. H. 149 cm. Nara, *c*. 734.

74, 75 (*left*) Basū-sen (detail), (*right*) Mawara-nyō (detail), both by Tankei. Painted wood. Early 13th century.

indulge in self-centred fears or regrets, but to cultivate instead the samurai values of asceticism and selflessness. This tendency was given a great boost with the arrival of Chan Buddhism from China.

Zen Buddhism

As contact with China was resumed, increasing numbers of Japanese reformist Buddhist masters like Eisai (1141–1215) and Dōgen (1200–1253), studied there and brought back the self-reliant teaching known as Chan (or Zen in Japanese). It was ascetic and pragmatic, and eschewed all external rituals. This no-nonsense approach held a strong appeal for the Japanese warrior class and soon found official patronage. Zen monasteries in Chinese style were founded in quick succession, the Kenninji (1202) and Tōfukuji (1243) in Kyoto, and the Kenchōji (1253) and Engakuji (1282) in Kamakura.

Although Zen teaching stressed the futility of extraneous intellectual and artistic activity, there was gradually built up a corpus of poems and ink paintings used by Zen masters to demonstrate various aspects of enlightenment. While these products may on occasion jolt the recipient into a degree of enlightenment, they proved a double-edged sword: playing as they did on the practitioner's desire for perfection in poetry or painting, they risked distracting him from his Path.

A genre of patriarchal portraiture, *chinzō*, often charting a master's active life, flourished with the proliferation of Zen monasteries. *Chinzō* represents the essential personal and direct transmission of the Law. A portrait of the master, with an appropriate inscription of dedication, was given to the disciple only when he had achieved a measure of enlightenment. It acknowledged the bond of *karma* which formed an important part of the disciple's life. Many portraits of famous Chinese masters were brought back by grateful Japanese disciples; the personal messages 'from Mind to Mind' strengthened the disciple's spiritual self-control. Jan Fontein and Money Hickman have observed that 'there is perhaps no other form of Chinese and Japanese art in which painting and calligraphy are so intimately connected in their purpose and meaning.'

In 1246 the great Southern Song Chan master Lanqi Daolong (1213–78) arrived in Japan. Two years later he went to Kamakura and converted the Hōjō regent Tokiyori. A magnificent monastery, Kenchōji, was built on the slopes just north of the city and was inaugurated in 1253 with Daolong as its founding abbot. This was the first purely Chinese Chan ritual ever held in Japan. With shōgunal patronage Zen quickly spread throughout Japan. A portrait of Lanqi Daolong in the Kenchōji, by an unknown   76 Japanese painter, shows the founder about seven years before his death. He is seated in the master's high chair, feet tucked under his habit, holding

76 Portrait of Lanqi Daolong (1213–1278) (detail). Silk hanging scroll, with colophon by Daolong dated 1271.

113

77 *Minamoto no Yoritomo* by Fujiwara Takanobu (1142–1205). Hanging scroll; ink, colour on silk. 12th century.

78 Portrait of Emperor Hanazono, by Goshin. Hanging scroll; ink, colours on paper. 1338.

his staff and observing the world attentively with benign yet stern eyes. He looks young for his age, nearly seventy; despite his slight and bony frame, his skin is clear and firm. The fluid, undulating ink brush-strokes show direct Song influence as does the coloration in transparent washes of dark and light browns. A new era of Chinese culture is launched, in spite of strict Chan injunctions against attachment, even attachment to culture.

Kamakura painting

The clear-sighted Zen view of the world injected a striking new realism into Japanese portraiture of the period. Some early examples are the set of portraits in Jingoji temple in Kyoto, attributed to Fujiwara Takanobu (1142–1205). The portrait of the Shōgun Minamoto no Yoritomo is still tinged with some Heian opacity and formality. It had been considered rude in Heian times to copy a person's likeness. But here the artist has not hesitated to bring out his subject's thick lips, protruding mouth suggesting buck teeth, small ear-lobes, flat cranium and slightly rounded, narrow nose and, above all, his vehement and ruthless personality. The cold, fierce eyes, for example, partially closed, borrow from the convention used in depicting angry Buddhist deities. The 'single lines' are in fact built up from a series of hair-fine brush-strokes. The black figured brocade, red

77

inner collar, gold scabbard, ivory tablet of state and gold-encrusted front sash are still opaque, in conformity with Heian practice, but the eyelids, nostrils, ears and lips are discreetly shaded to suggest real dimensions.

Takanobu was famous for realistic rendering; he painted only the faces of his subjects, leaving the rest to specialists. In 1173, a courtier recorded in his diary that Takanobu's mural of the Emperor and his court was so life-like that he, the courtier, was able to recognize everyone and thanked the Gods that he himself had not been present at the occasion – a clear example of the Heian aversion to life-like portraiture. It is significant, even so, that this same group portrait was commissioned by the Emperor Go-Shirakawa-in himself. Although opposition courtiers described the painting as coarse and dreary, and closed the building in which it was housed, the allure of realism proved irresistible. By the early thirteenth century, many more painted records of this type had been commissioned by the palace and courtiers were even identified on the paintings by their names and ages.

Another example of the informal but penetrating style is the revealing fourteenth-century portrait by Goshin, a descendant of Takanobu, of the Emperor Hanazono (1297–1348). It is painted in ink on paper and washed in transparent colours. The emperor abdicated in 1318 and took Buddhist vows in 1334. A highly erudite man, he is shown here at the age of forty-two, in a grey monk's habit, holding a rosary and a fan, gazing wearily at

78

the world. A patchwork brocade mantle, with a golden chrysanthemum and grasses on a white ground, offsets the clerical habit. The face is a scholar's, sensitive and effete; Hanazono himself paid tribute to the realism of the painting by inscribing on it, left, 'My deplorable nature, painted by Goshin in the Autumn of 1338.'

Muromachi ink painting

Through patronage of Zen monasteries and associated cultural activities, the martial rulers in Kamakura sought to produce a cultural legacy to rival that of the aristocratic Fujiwara, and thus to establish legitimacy. They patronized Zen monastries which were centres of Chinese learning; in time, some Japanese monks became so absorbed in Chinese literature, scholarship and arts that they came to be chastised as *bunjinsō* or '*literati* monks'. Many spent long years in China and the quality and character of their artistic output often approached that of Chinese Chan monks and *literati*. Although Chan teachings held a profound appeal for the Japanese, the Chinese language, script and ink monochrome painting were alien at best, anathema at worst, and shōgunal promotion of Chinese culture proved to be, for Japanese artist-monks, a formidable task.

Throughout the Yuan dynasty in China, the Chan School was an international community with frequent and enthusiastic exchanges across the Yellow Sea. Chinese abbots were invited to found Japanese Zen monasteries and Japanese monks went to study in China, some eventually becoming abbots there. Chinese poetry and calligraphy by Japanese monks such as Sesson Yūbai (1290–1346) were highly regarded in both countries. Another painter-monk, Mokuan Reien (*fl.* 1330s–1345), who went to China about 1329, became primate of a Chinese monastery.

79 In the *Four Sleepers* Mokuan portrays a favourite Chan theme: the legendary eccentrics, Hanshan and Shide, with Fenggan and his tiger, all soundly asleep. The younger men, Hanshan and Shide, have been identified in later writings as avatars of the bodhisattvas Mañjuśrī and Samantabhadra. (The Chan School added the mounted Fenggan and created its own trinity.) Mokuan's style reveals a full grasp of Chinese ink wash techniques in the fluid descriptive lines, and wet areas where darker ink is allowed to blur, the extremely dry brush in shading Fenggan's face and belly, and the use of fine, almost invisible, lines for all the facial features. This style is a development of the Southern Song Chan ink painting tradition, 'apparition painting', *wanglianghua* (Japanese *mōryōga*).

While Mokuan was in China, the seat of power shifted from Kamakura. In 1368, Ashikaga Yoshimitsu (ruled 1368–94) from the Muromachi

老豊干抱虎睏拾詩
寒山打作一蹇儌湯火
夢裏囻流依之老
樹
寒巖底
祥寿紹宏拜手

79 *Four Sleepers* by Mokuan
Reien, inscribed by Xiangfu
Shaomi. Hanging scroll; ink on
paper. 14th century.

district in Kyoto became the new Shōgun. Unlike Minamoto no
Yoritomo, who disdained court life, Yoshimitsu was determined to rival
it in both culture and opulence. In the Kamakura period, the restoration of
Buddhist monasteries destroyed in the civil war had had priority. In the
Muromachi period, the Shōgun promoted Chinese-style ink painting,
pavilions, gardens and tea-houses as aesthetic alternatives to the imperial
taste for Japanese culture.

Due to restrictive Ming policies, Japanese monastic artists now had to work without living and studying in China or having guidance from Chinese masters. This vital missing link accounts for the peculiarly unfulfilled character of Muromachi art in its Chinese oriented works. Although, through most of the fourteenth century, Zen traffic to China had been brisk and scholarship intense, Japanese monasteries had not established Chinese-style *ateliers* to ensure proper transmission of Zen-related art – understandable in a philosophy which eschewed sutras and icons. The artistic Chan repertory of Yuan China had consisted in general of highly abbreviated ink monochrome representations of men, orchids, bamboo, pines, or landscapes which summed up well known motifs in a few strokes. Japanese artists were thus confronted with the pictorial equivalent of shorthand but without recourse to the fuller script. This first serious encounter with China's ink painting coincided with its evolution towards yet further abbreviation, verging on formal dissolution. Chan works of a wide range of quality now entered Japan, from poor to sublime. The Japanese artist could either slavishly copy his continental model or adapt it.

The latter option, though more suited to the creative impulse, was restricted by the need for iconographical fidelity. Since Chinese Chan works expressed spontaneous exhilaration or insight, the Japanese artist had to enliven his version with a degree of inspiration and freedom but could not inject any different vision of his own. His artistic inclinations could not fully surface, but were inevitably routed through the medium of incompatible Chinese models. This was particularly true after the Ming restoration of 1368, when travel to and from China was curtailed.

While outwardly adhering to the continental vocabulary, to comply with iconographic or shōgunal demands, Japanese Zen ink painting was nevertheless being slowly transformed into a more poetic and indigenous expression. This was achieved by altering the morphology and expression of the models but without changing compositional elements. Thus, Muromachi ink painting was deprived of the complete artistic freedom which had marked the development in the Heian period of Tang blue and green styles into *Yamato-e*. And for viewers today, it may lack the totality of transformation and fulfilment so apparent in *onna-e* painting, *onnade* calligraphy, *raku* pottery, *Rimpa* painting and calligraphy or *ukiyo-e* woodblock prints, genres where Japan's artistic genius was given fullest expression.

However, rearrangement of Chinese elements in a Japanese manner was not only possible, but inevitable. In *Orchids*, Gyokuen Bompō (1348–1420) demonstrates that a poetic version of China's philosophical

80

80 *Orchids* by Gyokuen Bompō.
Hanging scroll; ink on paper. Late 14th
century.

prototype can be successfully made without changing motifs or technique. (Bompō was a *literatus* or *bunjinsō* and once served as abbot of
Nanzenji in Kyoto. He was celebrated as a poet and calligrapher but above
all for his orchid paintings.) In this painting, the standard rocks and plants
are depicted; but instead of radiating outwards to capture and control
space, as is often the case in Chinese orchid paintings, Bompō's elements,

81 Golden Pavilion, Kyoto, 1398. (The original was destroyed by fire in 1950 and rebuilt in 1964.)

82 *White-robed Kannon* with flanking landscapes by Ue Gukei. Hanging scrolls; ink
on silk. Late 14th century.

in gentle and fluid strokes of graded ink wash, enfold an open and mobile
space which is charged with peculiar psychic energy.

While the genre of orchids, bamboo, etc., in ink derived specifically
from scholarly Yuan Chan sources, other Japanese works produced under
Zen influence are of diverse origins and show a marked degree of
eclecticism and syncretism. A good example is the triptych by Ue Gukei   82
(*fl.* 1361–75), showing a White-robed Kannon flanked by landscapes.
Although landscapes were known to form the backdrop of patriarchal and
arhat paintings, this is the earliest example of a triptych where landscape is
brought forward in such a dramatic manner. There is an ebullience,
perhaps inspired by Korean models, and the abbreviated brush technique
suggests familiarity with the work of the Southern Song master, Yujian.
In the central panel the ingenuous Kannon floats placidly on a rock which

121

fairly erupts from the water, while to the right and left mountains, trees and rocks rush, uprooted, towards the figure in the central panel. The artist's interest here is not in stability, solidity or spatial clarity; instead, he shows an illusionistic landscape swirling with gravity-defying motion, while each of the three figures, the Kannon, woodsman and fisherman, is utterly absorbed, oblivious of the commotion.

One of the most accomplished monk painters was Ryōzen (fl. mid-fourteenth century) who may have come from Kyushu. All his works are of Buddhist subjects and suggest a busy, professional painter of considerable attainment, surprising in a monk thought to have held high ecclesiastic rank. One of his best known paintings is of a white heron. Although ostensibly a secular subject, various bird species were used symbolically in Zen painting. Here the heron, painted in white upon the ink-washed paper, is caught mid-step just as it stoops forward, recoiling its long neck in preparation for the lunge at an unseen fish. In the right foreground a few reeds and leaves balance the tension created at the left. Ryōzen's brushwork in the fine, fluid water lines, the feather and beak strokes and the more impulsive upward strokes of the reeds is masterly. In this simple picture, doubtless based on continental models, Ryōzen has achieved the intensity and purity which are characteristic goals of Zen meditation.

Gardens and landscape painting

By 1265 Tenryūji temple had been completed on the site, to the northwest of Kyoto, of an ancient garden which had been a favourite retreat of courtiers since the tenth century. A remarkable rock arrangement in the pond, suggesting the Chinese isle of immortals, Penglai, may well have been constructed by visiting Chinese craftsmen. The seven stones create a three-dimensional Song landscape – a soaring central pinnacle, flanked by subordinate peaks – and may well be the only extant example of Song rock-garden art.

The collection of Chinese works and their reinterpretation, hitherto purely a monastic activity, was now enthusiastically encouraged by the Shōgun. Ashikaga Yoshimitsu (who died in 1408) bought an ancient estate renowed for its garden and built a splendid study now known as the Kinkaku or Golden Pavilion, which he used for reading and the enjoyment of his art collection. The Heian pond garden, originally designed to be viewed as changing perspectives as one progressed in a moving boat, could now be seen in its entirety and from a single vantage-point, his three-storey pavilion. The emphasis in this static view of the

83 *White Heron* by Ryōzen. Ink on paper. Mid-14th century.

84 Penglai, the immortals' isle. Rock arrangement in the pond garden of Tenryūji, Kyoto. Completed by 1265.

garden art has shifted from the Heian idea of social boating parties to one of quiet, Zen oriented contemplation.

The Shōguns not only collected and displayed Chinese Chan-related art originally imported by and for Japanese monasteries, but also made a collection of Chinese Imperial Academy works related to Southern Song court painting in an attempt at parity with the Emperor. (In 1382, for example, Yoshimitsu ordered the building of the Shōkokuji monastery, and employed its painter-monks to decorate his own manor as well.) In this way Zen-related art works, once the creations of the spontaneous exhilaration of erudite clerics for their mutual appreciation, came to assume a secular and ornamental function.

In the late fourteenth century, reflecting the secularization among Chan monks in China and Korea where literary accomplishment replaced spiritual quest, a form of poem painting (*shigajiku*) evolved; in it, landscape painting complements the group of poems composed during a gathering of literary monks. It had been largely the product of monastic literary associations until a Shōgun, probably Yoshimitsu, specifically ordered such a work to be produced as a backdrop screen for his dais. He asked distinguished monks from Kyotó to compose poems, and commissioned Josetsu (*fl.* early fifteenth century) of his Shōkokuji monastery to paint in the 'new style' (of the Southern Song academician and Chan painter Liang Kai). The theme of the painting was the Zen riddle on catching the slippery catfish with the smooth-skinned gourd. Josetsu's compelling work is largely in monochrome, with a touch of red to accent the gourd. The Liang Kai manner can be seen in the hooked and angular lines of the drapery. The sweep of the bank is remarkable, from the dense confluence of streams on the left to the opening up to grand dissolution on the right (a reversal of the usual narrative flow from right to left). The gentle curves of bank, bamboo, catfish, gourd and flowing water are offset by the bristling intensity of the reeds on the right, and by the extraordinary face of the aspirant. This screen was subsequently re-mounted in its present hanging scroll format.

'Studio paintings' which portray an idealized mountain retreat also appeared as *shigajiku*. *Reading in the Bamboo Studio* is by Josetsu's pupil Shūbun (*fl.* 1423–58), who in turn taught the great Sesshū. Shūbun further developed the current monastic 'mind-landscape' style. He retained Southern Song elements which enhance the sense of expanding space (houses and boats sunk deeply among trees and reeds, mists which separate planes, reduced figures walking hunched over), and thus 'archaized' the Chinese models then becoming available. Just as Bompō transformed the orchid, so Shūbun turned the increasingly solid forms

85

86, 88

85 *Catching Catfish with a Gourd* by Josetsu. Hanging scroll; ink, colour on paper. Early 15th century.

and closed space of Yuan and Ming works in the Xia Gui tradition into evocative, almost transparent forms embracing a fluid space that appears to breathe and expand in the mist. The scholar-monk looks out from his thatched hermitage on to the real subject of the painting: poetic space/time (here enfolded by langorous pines and, on the other side of the lake, by the outjutting banks and ring of misty mountains).

Poetic spatial expanse achieves dramatic dimensions in the *Small Lake* 87 *Landscape* by a follower of the Shūbun School, Shōkei Tenyū (*fl.* 1440–60). More assertive brushwork, however, here robs the motif of some of its dreaminess, and the gold coloured pavilions inject a note of formality. The water expanse is more vast, opening to the left and right and merging with the sky in the upper left.

86 (*overleaf*)) *Reading in the Bamboo Studio* (detail) by Shūbun. Hanging scroll; ink on paper. Muromachi, mid-15th century. (See pl. 88)

87 (*overleaf*) *Small Lake Landscape* by Shōkei Tenyū. Hanging scroll; ink, colours on paper. Mid-15th century.

面水好山皆可廬
唯多竹雪稱吾居
應言門非是嚴佳宅
日課猶愁欠讀書

村菴靈兆

88 *Reading in the Bamboo Studio,*
complete scroll showing the poetic
inscriptions by six monks. (See
pl. 86)

89 *West Lake* by Bunsei, inscribed by Zuikei Shūhō
and Ichijō Kanera. Hanging scroll; ink on paper.
Before 1473.

One of the most lyrical extant works of the period is *West Lake* by Bunsei (*fl.* 1460s), a mature statement of the Shūbun 'mind-landscape' ideal. Like Tenyū and Shūbun before him, Bunsei worked with Yuan and Ming works in the Xia Gui style, keeping in mind Southern Song notions of scale, and arranged elements from diverse sources in a Japanese formal and spatial relationship. As good Chinese works were scarce and spanned some 250 years, and as the Shōgun often specified that Chinese styles should be followed, it became common practice among Muromachi painters to produce highly eclectic works incorporating not only vignettes from various Chinese sources, but also the structural changes made at different periods. It is also noteworthy that while most of the Chinese sources were in the intimate format of fan paintings, album leaves or horizontal handscrolls (favoured in Southern Song and Yuan), works of the time were mostly narrow, vertical hanging scrolls (fashionable in contemporary Ming) or large-scale sliding door paintings (*fusuma-e*) and screens (*byōbu*). In Bunsei's working of vignettes from different Chinese compositions into a coherent vertical format, we see Japanese genius at work. In the quiet, contemplative space of the mind-landscape we see the scholarly equivalent of the 'emotive cloud' found in Heian *Yamato-e* painting. Not so passionate, the mood is nature-oriented and more profound, the space flowing in a generous S-curve to the middle left and then up to the right. Elements from Xia Gui landscape prototypes are laid out along a consistent groundplane. Each group of motifs is consistent within itself, but the diminution of the bridge section in the foreground in relation to the rock and twin pines draws the entire scene together and creates a hush which reverberates from vignette to vignette.

The Shōgun also collected works associated with the scholar-amateur tradition later called the Southern School in China. Unlike the 'Northern' academic landscapes, which feature jagged rocks painted in slanted 'axe' strokes, the Southern '*literati*' landscapes derive from a tradition of rounded hills and expansive lake vistas, where the texturing was done largely with a more upright brush in ropey 'hemp-fibre' strokes. In Muromachi collections this Southern style is represented by works associated with the Chan monk Muqi (who died between 1269 and 1274), including Buddhist figures, animals, flowers and landscapes. Most Japanese landscapists worked in the Northern academy style, but one of the Shōgun's curators, Sōami (who died in 1525), was able to produce works in the Southern style, such as the breathtaking *Eight Views of the Xiao and Xiang* on the sliding door panels of the Daisenin sub-temple of the Daitokuji monastery. These incorporate major features of the Chinese literati traditions related to the Song masters Juran and Mi Youren. (The

90 *Eight Views of the Xiao and Xiang* by Sōami. Detail of one of 23 sliding door panels in Muqi style. Early 16th century.

Ami family had for generations acted as curators, conservators, appraisers and connoisseurs for the Ashikaga, and Sōami had grown up in the sinophile milieu of Yoshimasa's court, acquiring intimate knowledge of Chinese painting styles from direct study.) This large work, spanning over twenty panels, demonstrates Sōami's understanding of the Chinese *literati* mode, and shows the greater suitability of the Southern mode for Japanese expression. None the less, shōgunal preference for academic styles precluded the development in Japan of a Southern style. This development had to wait till the Tokugawa period when independent painters took it up on their own.

90   In the detail shown, originally on one of the western sliding doors but now remounted in hanging scroll format, Sōami achieves a fine synthesis of Chinese Southern imagery and technique with Japanese setting and

130

91 Portrait of Zen master Ikkyū Sōjun by Bokusai. Hanging scroll; ink, colours on paper. Late 14th century.

expression. Low-lying, rolling hills swathed in rising autumnal mists yield to marshy grasslands where boats are moored and geese descend in formation. There is a striking resemblance to the half dormant, half waking mood of the *Early spring landscape* among the Phoenix Hall murals   57
(p. 79). The houses tucked beneath the mountain are wrapped in quiet; only the occasional wild goose breaks the silence of the chilly air. Two boats are moored among the reeds in the middleground and two fishermen by the lowest bank are all but lost in the vast, evening calm. Like an emotive cloud, the expanding mist is free-form, rising, all enveloping. Sōami's composition is mid-way between the void-centred works of the Shūbun School, and the mass-centred works of the Sesshū School to follow. His mastery of the Southern idiom with soft, pliant texture strokes, wet, inky one-line tree trunks, and the consummate use of inkwash in the evanescent mists make this – the earliest example of *nanga* or Southern-style landscape created in Japan – one of the master-pieces of Japanese ink painting.

Portraiture, meanwhile, continued to be vigorously realistic. The great Zen master, Ikkyū Sōjun (1394–1481), was of royal birth and began Buddhist studies as a boy. He attained advanced spiritual learning, and refused the abbacy of the Daitokuji because of its administrative corruption. In his portrait by Bokusai, painted during his lifetime, he is   91
depicted with economy of line and great sensitivity. Bokusai concentrates

on the worn, thoughtful face and, in particular, on suggesting the Master's penetrating mind.

The intense cultural activities of Kyoto were not lost on provincial rulers, *daimyō*, and the later fifteenth century saw the growth of regional patronage and art collections. The greatest master of Japanese ink landscape, Sesshū Tōyō (1420–1506) came from this regional tradition. Having studied Zen painting at the Shōkokuji in Kyoto under Shūbun, he founded the Unkoku-an studio at the south-western tip of Japan's main island, close to the Chinese trade route. From 1467 to 1469, he accompanied a trade mission to China, where he plunged into feverish activity, painting a mural in Peking, sketching the countryside and directly experiencing Ming academic painting. This exposure to the massiveness, solidity and relative self-sufficiency of Chinese painting *in situ* profoundly altered Sesshū's own vision. On his return to Japan, he replaced the spatial ambiguity and inconsistencies of scale which had characterized the poetic Shūbun style with a substantive, rational order. In a very late work, however, paying tribute to his Japanese teacher, 92 he nostalgically returned to traditional Shūbun motifs. But the focus of the work has moved from empty space to solid masses. The dominant feature is the central mountain. The viewer's response is no longer to drift in reverie but to follow the measured steps of the travellers. They wend their way from the stone path, lower left, around the foreground boulder, past pavilions tucked beneath the road, to the rocky promontory and pavilion on the left where they will gaze past the jutting peaks on to the lake. However, the twin pines which used to enfold Shūbun's space now obliterate the lake expanse with their central position and assertive, upward surge. By the time of this work Sesshū had already startled the world with his virile granite forms (such as the famous *Autumn* and *Winter* landscapes) in his personal version of the Xia Gui style, the explosive renditions of the splattered ink landscape works after Yujian (*fl.* thirteenth century), and the introduction of his interpretation of the Yuan master Gao Kegong. But here he recalls the poetic legacy of his Japanese teachers, even though his emphasis on physical reality has indelibly marked the age.

Sesshū's legacy flourished in various styles. His favourite pupil at the Unkoku-an was Sōen (*fl.* 1489–1500), who received the master's famous *haboku* (splattered ink) landscape as certificate of his proficiency in the 93 style. In Sōen's own *haboku* landscape the handling of brushwork and ink is far closer to Sesshū than to Shūbun or the original Southern Song master Yujian. More poetic than Sesshū's works, the organization of space is nevertheless conditioned by mass and motion. The mist-

92 *Landscape* by Sesshū Tōyō,
inscribed by Ryōan Keigo in 1507.
Hanging scroll; ink and light
colours on paper. 15th century.

93 *Haboku* landscape by Sōen. Ink on
paper. Late 15th or early 16th century

94 *Evening Snow* from *Eight Views of the Xiao and Xiang* by Tōshun. One of eight hanging scrolls; ink on paper. Early 16th century.

engirdled central range twists into the picture plane in an S-curve, while an arrow-straight boat heads for the centre from the left, and a firm plank bridge brings in (potential) motion from the right. All forces converge at the central foreground in a dynamic thrust of jet black strokes. This is in direct opposition to the dispersing nature of Shūbun School works.

94   Another follower of Sesshū, Tōshun (*fl.* 1506–42), echoes the master's sense of turbulence in a splattered ink version of Yujian's views of the *Xiao and Xiang*. Instead of the Southern Song master's inwardness and quiescence, Tōshun's work is closer to Sesshū's in both brush technique and expression. The snow mountain on the left is reserved in white, while a waterfall flows from a crevice over snow-covered rocks. A wintry gale is blowing snow towards the mountain across a darkening sky. This is no scene of poetic wandering; mass and motion rule.

95   With the waning of Ashikaga fortunes and restlessness of regional rulers, art works of the later fifteenth century imbue the sense of motion with a foreboding of violence, and increasingly reflect a martial mien. Sesson Shūkei (*c.* 1504–89) was active largely in northeastern Japan; his famous *Hawk on Pine* perfectly captures the aggressive mood of the time. Done in rapid ink strokes, the work centres on the bird of prey; bristling

95 *Hawk on Pine* by Sesson Shūkei. One of a pair of hanging scrolls; ink on paper. Mid-16th century.

tension charges the entire conception, down to the last pine needle. In a
96   late work, *Landscape in Wind*, Sesson depicts a solid world in turmoil. His
mature style is brilliant in its total fusion of modelling strokes (which had
erstwhile merely adhered) to the forms. His remarkable integration of
description with expression reveals a new, idiosyncratic vocabulary of
volatile forms marked by rocks resembling solid projectiles which pierce
the space with new violence. Here a startling contrast of stillness and
motion, perhaps of peace and war, is evoked by the juxtaposition of the
moonlit islet jutting from tranquil waters on the left, with the mighty
central rocks whose energy charges at gale force, bending the trees and
grasses and virtually dissolving the mass in the process. The fisherman
seems incongruous, attempting his daily chore in all the commotion.

97   The *Dry Landscape* garden in Ryōanji, Kyoto, though by contrast a
monument to stillness, nevertheless sums up all the artistic tensions of the
Muromachi age. This Zen garden, framed by a wall and meant to be
viewed from the veranda of the adjoining building, creates a seascape
using only rocks (for mountains) and white pebbles (sea). Seventeen rocks
are arranged in five groups amidst the raked (wavy) pebbles to produce

96 *Landscape in Wind* by Sesson Shūkei. Hanging scroll; ink on paper. Late
16th century.

97 Dry landscape garden in Ryōanji, Kyoto, constructed in the 1480s.

maximum visual tension. Viewed from the entrance, the largest group is in the foreground while the others decrease in size as they increase in distance: it is a brilliant use of built-in perspective to make the modest space appear far larger. To change the position of a single rock would dissipate the psychological energy so generated. This supreme statement of reality/illusion has been the despair of successive generations of garden masters vainly trying to repeat the effect in other settings, and has remained a major challenge for scholars of the history of Japanese gardens.

CHAPTER SIX

Azuchi-Momoyama and Edo (1576-1868)

Castle murals

In 1576, Oda Nobunaga seized control of Japan, and made Azuchi into a stronghold centred on a walled castle, the whole completed in 1579. (In these times, many ambitious men built fortified castles on enormous stone ramparts, their stone walls pierced by small windows and topped by massive timbers.) Interior walls of the Azuchi castle were decorated by members of the prolific studio led by Kanō Eitoku (1543–90). The completion of the Azuchi castle marks the start of the Azuchi-Momoyama period, named after the castle-towns of the contending warlords.

The Kanō painters, who had never been monks, had been in the service of the Shōgun for several generations, and by the Edo period were creating the official style for the Tokugawa shōgunate. Although most of the great castles have now long been destroyed, Kanō Eitoku's work can still be seen in monasteries such as the Jukōin sub-temple of Daitokuji in 98 Kyoto. Works like *Pine and Crane* display the young artist's virtuosity in brushwork, in the handling of form; they also demonstrate the ebullience and martial vigour characteristic of the age. Eitoku, working here in the Southern style of Muqi (once so perfectly japanized by Sōami) has transformed the distant subject's soft parallel modelling strokes and gentle moss dots into bristling, angular configurations of rocky shores and massive craggy pines that dominate the space. The crackling tension is nearly audible. His forms fill the large sliding doors and extend implicitly beyond them.

99 The small windows of castles such as Himeji encouraged screen painting on gold surfaces to help reflect light into the dark rooms: entire walls and ceilings were ornately decorated in this way. Kanō masters spent much time creating imposing, heroic designs in impasto, such as the 100 magnificent *Great Pine* murals. These are by the hand, or school, of Kanō Tanyū (1602–74). Room after room, hall after hall, was decorated with paintings of Chinese curly-maned lions, Zen dragons and tigers, the four seasons, moored boats and curved bridges, gardens and peonies, all executed in encrusted pigments and lavishly finished in gold foil. To

98 *Pine and Crane* by Kanō Eitoku. Sliding door panels; ink on paper. 1566.

convince the masses that he was there to stay, Hideyoshi, the new warlord, exploited every means of self-aggrandizement: once, for example, he gave a mass tea party, lasting for several days, to no less than five thousand guests.

The art of mural decoration is rooted in the traditions of Japanese painting. Even if one ignores the cave paintings of the Tumulus period, professional painting on a large scale had begun as early as the eighth century, with the decoration of Hōryūji. Heian domestic architecture included many large paintings on screens which functioned as movable walls and which became a firmly established interior feature with the invention of the sliding door (*fusuma*). Almost nothing of these early works remains apart from a few landscape screens and, if it had not been for the meticulous detail of interior scenes depicted in narrative hand scrolls surviving from each century, the modern viewer could suppose that mural painting was a late phenomenon in Japan.

The usual Momoyama wall coverings were sumptuous paintings of flowers, landscapes or figures upon gold foil walls or sliding doors. In *White Peonies* by Kanō Sanraku (1559–1635), even the petals and leaves show the characteristic glitter, ostentation and extroversion of the age. 101

99 Himeji castle with stone ramparts, Hyōgo Prefecture. Late 16th century.

100 *Great Pine* murals, Nijō castle, Kyoto. School of Kanō Tanyū, 1624–26.

101 *White Peonies* by Kanō Sanraku. Detail of sliding door panels; colours and *impasto* on gold foil. Early 17th century.

One of the most remarkable painters of the Edo period was Kanō Tanyū, grandson of Eitoku. He worked in both Edo and Kyoto and produced paintings for the imperial palace and for the Shōgun's castle in Nagoya. The green and gold pines in Nijō castle in Kyoto are generally thought to be his work. In 1636 he painted *Legends of the Tōshōgū Shrine* at Nikkō, handling the delicate Tosa hand scroll style with ease. Tanyū helped reinvigorate the court-favoured Tosa tradition which was then on the point of dissolution from a half millennium's recycling of the same motifs.

Tanyū's insatiable interest in all manners of painting, whether Chinese or Japanese, resulted in the first collection of art-historical records of works he had seen. Scroll after scroll contains concise notes and reduced sketches (*shukuzu*) which not only reproduce general outlines but also accurately reflect the original brushwork. This tradition of recording works was continued by Tanyū's followers and 'Kanō *shukuzu*' are an invaluable resource for art historians today.

In the mural *Night Fishing with Cormorants* Tanyū casts a keen and sympathetic eye over his contemporary world. It is night and the scene is

102

lit by torches from boats forming a semicircle in the bay. A rich merchant, top left, sits enjoying the lively scene of rippling water, diving cormorants and busy fishermen, while an elder regales him with stories. The interest in this scene is in the diverse poses of this activity; the surrounding rocks and reeds are sketched economically, in gentle hues, in contrast to Tanyū's usually more formal style.

Tanyū's visual experience was among the broadest of his time, as he had access to imperial and shōgunal collections of ancient and contemporary works, both Chinese and Japanese. As their study-sketches of works included those by Chinese masters of the Southern *literati* School, he and his followers could have produced works in this idiom, had they wished, but the orthodox shōgunal style had long been set either in the formal four-square Ma-Xia idiom or in the nearly brushless, abbreviated Yujian style in ink wash. Southern Painting in the manner of the Chinese idealist painters began elsewhere.

A lively native movement had been developing among the aristocracy and upper merchant class (*machishū*) during the fifteenth and sixteenth

102 *Night Fishing with Cormorants* by Kanō Tanyū. Six-fold screen. Mid-17th century.

centuries. Even the town painters, the anonymous screen decorators of the late Muromachi period, were producing great numbers of expanded landscapes based on *Yamato-e* painting. The subjects were the eternal Japanese themes: famous places with poetic associations, the four seasons, pines, reeds and boats. The sun and moon feature in some of the most remarkable works of all. In a work of the Tosa School, for example, the 103 four seasons are worked into a unified screen format with the winter scene appearing third in the sequence. On the right, a full, noon sun, golden over tall, round mountains bright with spring blooms, is the standard opening. The second group of mountains is shown in summer; at their feet the waves are turbulent. In the third section, the snow-covered folds of hills are contoured to balance the misty autumnal mountains further left. This layering of mountains in a frontal manner, an old *Yamato-e* device, can also be seen in the thirteenth-century *Amida Descending over the Mountains* (*Yamagoshi Amida*). Eighteenth-century Japanese theorists called this Japan's own blue-green landscape style. It had always survived in both monastic and secular painting, in spite of all the periods of Chinese dominance.

Evocative murals

Tawaraya Sōtatsu (who died in ?1643), the greatest master of evocative screen-painting, was bred in this delicate, archaizing tradition. Sōtatsu produced creative and original variations on the centuries-old themes. His *Matsushima* screens in the Freer Gallery, Washington DC, are one of his most striking works. This compelling image of a turbulent sea crashing onto small, pine-covered islets may be a view of Ise, the home of Japan's imperial shrine. However, Sōtatsu's rendition is less a rearrangement of well-worn forms than a completely new perception of their latent possibilities.

The theme of waves, rocks and pines had long been treated expertly on screens. The favourite Muromachi arrangement is to align the pine-topped rocks along the foreground, leaving the upper two thirds for the waves, interspersed by two or more protruding rocks. Sōtatsu's arrangement, three rocky isles and three sandy shoals across two screens, dramatically exploits these Heian motifs. Here, however, each element is seen from a different perspective. The largest rocky cliff, which leads in from the right, is seen from an elevated vantage point, while the middle and third cliffs, in diminution, are shown from increasingly lower perspectives while the middle one is seen frontally. The left-hand screen shows three sandbanks, the largest one on a flat, gold ground, extending into the right-hand screen, where it changes into a cloud. On the left-hand screen it is in fact shown from directly overhead and its two giant pines are laterally spread out to give a better view. Above and below, two shrub-covered sandy islands are depicted in an unprecedented mixture of ink, gold and silver paste. These islands too, seen from overhead, appear at this same time like floating clouds. (The only genuine cloud in the work extends from the top of the right-hand screen.) Once drawn into the picture, the viewer is taken on a somersault flight proceeding from the right. First he dives into the waves but is then hurled skyward over the beaches. The viewer becomes the playful plover (*namichidori*) conspicuously absent but implied. The waves are rendered throughout from the same 45-degree elevation; their whirlpools and rushing crests are in stark contrast to the stillness of the rocks and trees.

103 *Landscape with Sun and Moon*, anonymous, Tosa school. Right-hand screen (detail) of double six-fold screen; ink, colours and gold on paper. Mid-16th century.

Inkwash murals

Japanese artists had long perfected the use of inkwash to render atmospheric mist in fine gradations, and the use of long, curving lines over a large area. The Azuchi-Momoyama period saw the final triumph over this latest of Chinese artistic imports in the thorough japanization of ink monochrome painting. Artists now covered entire palace and monastery walls with continuous murals, as if wrapping the halls in giant hand scrolls. It was a common practice for rooms to be surrounded by the *Eight Views of Xiao and Xiang*, by giant trees or by stormy seas.

Pine and Plum by Moonlight is a superb example of the late style of Kaihō 104,105 Yūshō (1533–1615), an outstanding artist of the age. Twin curving streams emerge from the thick mists, which function as emotive clouds creating an evocative, expansive space. Pine and prunus trees flank the moonlit scene; half hidden by mist and branches, some dandelions and spring grasses can just be seen. In spite of the economy of line and the abbreviated rendering of forms, unctuous brush work gives the scene a

104, 105 *Pine and Plum by Moonlight* by Kaihō Yūshō. Pair of six-panel screens; ink and light colour on paper. Late 16th century.

striking, almost tactile reality. *Streams in Moonlight* is not only an eclectic synthesis of *Yamato-e* and *Rimpa* styles (see below) but an original masterpiece.

106,107 Perhaps the most extraordinary transformation of the ink monochrome idiom is the double six-fold screen *Pine Forest* by Hasegawa Tōhaku (1539–1610), most of whose other surviving works are of the colours-on-gold genre of the Kanō school. Having made extensive studies of the style of the Song master, Muqi, and particularly of his paintings of monkeys and cranes now in the Daitokuji, Tōhaku achieves in his *Pine* screen a superb synthesis of Chinese techniques and Japanese motifs. Four groups of beach pines, *hamamatsu*, are placed across the twelve panels. Nearly eighty-five per cent of the painting surface is left blank and yet the entire screen is suffused with a sense of the mists and quietness of an autumn dawn. Whereas Yamato-e painters usually showed the pines in twisting, curving forms, Tōhaku shows them tall and gaunt, using a straw brush on thin, coarse paper, varying the intensity of his ink from faint to dark in swift, sure strokes. In the distance, a snowy peak adds to the feeling of grandeur and calm. This scene does not reflect the interests and activities of warlords but the Way of Tea, the new contemplative fashion which is in such striking contrast to the gaudy splendour of the feudal court.

106, 107 *Pine Forest* by Hasegawa Tōhaku. Pair of six-panel screens; ink on paper. Late 16th century.

108, 109 *Matsushima* (*Pine Island*) by Tawaraya Sōtatsu. Double six-panel screen; ink and colours on gold paper. Early 17th century.

The Way of Tea

Perhaps to counter his tendency to extravagance, Hideyoshi engaged as his mentor the most distinguished tea-master of the wealthy Sakai merchant class, Sen no Rikyū (1521–91). Rikyū's spartan views on the Way of Tea have since had a profound influence on both 'tea architecture' and on Japanese aesthetics as a whole.

Drinking tea in quiet surroundings had been instituted by the fifteenth-century tea-master Shukō in the time of the aesthete Shōgun Yoshimasa. He invented the ceremony of tea as an art form to be enjoyed in a small room specially designed for it, containing selected 'tea' paintings, calligraphy scrolls or Chinese celadons. Sen no Rikyū eschewed the jade-like perfection of celadons and favoured rough-textured and irregular peasant ware. He promoted spiritual ideals of 'harmony, respect, purity and tranquillity' and in 1582 built his tea room, the Tai-an, in a hut in his native Yamazaki. This small cedar structure is simple and rustic, based on asymmetric and irregular forms, with rough-textured earthen walls, unpolished, exposed beams, a cedar-board covered ceiling of two levels and papered windows of different shapes set at different heights above the seated guests' heads. The guest was invited to leave his worldly concerns outside with his sword, to crawl into the teahouse by the waist-high wriggling-in-opening (*nigiri guchi*), and to enter the warm, dark and intimate atmosphere. In this timeless world, friends commune, collected, at ease and in close proximity where the tea master's every move becomes one's own. In a recessed alcove, the host might choose to focus attention on a specially treasured art work or on an allusive floral arrangement which may induce 'spiritual one-pointedness'. To this day tea men maintain that it is a unique aesthetic experience which integrates the spirit of Zen, the beauty of art and of mundane things.

For his tea bowls, Rikyū commissioned the tile maker Chōjirō (1516–92) to produce *raku* ware. His rejection of Song celadons in favour of simple peasant ware produced the aesthetic which Okakura Tenshin has termed 'Japan's worship of the imperfect'. The irregular glaze, shape and decoration of *raku* was intended to echo the asymmetry of the teahouse as a whole; it was also felt that dazzling decoration on pottery would break the contemplative mood. Chōjirō's celebrated tea bowl *Katsujishi* is typical. It has a straight edge but an irregular mouth and foot, tapers slightly at the sides and rises upwards from the base to allow a clear view

110

110 *Katsujishi, raku* ware tea-bowl by Tanaka Chōjirō. Black slip glaze. H. 8.8, diam. 10.9 cm. 16th century.

111 *Myōkian*, tea house by Sen no Rikyū, 1582. Embedded stones lead to the entrance and the windows are framed by bamboo and wistaria.

112 *Tai-an* tea room of *Myōkian* tea house. (Notice recessed *tokonoma* alcove and two-level, cedar-board ceiling.)

of the foot-rim. The entire bowl is glazed in a dull matt black slip of irregular density, permitting the body's buff colour to lighten the tone in certain areas and to highlight its rough, pitted quality.

Although the smallness of Rikyū's Tai-an tea room did not have lasting influence, the *sukiya* style of architecture based on its aesthetic developed into a major tradition which eventually extended to domestic architecture, with or without a teahouse. Like *onna-e* painting, *onnade* calligraphy and *waka* poetry, the teahouse was a personal art form, catering to the intense Japanese need for the preservation of the private self as distinct from the public face. Both demand expression in art forms as in life styles. (Hideyoshi himself reflects the extremes. At one moment he would indulge in public displays of wealth and in the next he would crawl humbly into the darkness and intimacy of Rikyū's teahouse.)

The contrast between public and private architecture is nowhere better seen than in the ostentatious vulgarity of the shōgunal Nikkō Tōshōgū on the one hand and the pure taste of the detached imperial villa Katsura on the other. Both date from the early seventeenth century. The first

113
114

113 Yōmei-mon (Sunlight Gate), Nikkō Tōshōgū in Nikkō. Early 17th century.

114 *Katsura*, villa and garden of Prince Hachijō Toshihito. 1642.

Tokugawa Shōgun ordered a family shrine-mausoleum to be constructed in mountainous Nikkō. Every surface of this monumental project is lavishly decorated in painted relief or in lacquer and gold work. By contrast, the aristocracy having rarely felt the need for self-assertion, Prince Hachijō Toshihito and his son Noritada created in the Katsura imperial villa an idealized private world: cedar-roofed buildings, ponds and a garden designed to be walked in and enjoyed from different vantage-points at different seasons. Like the Tai-an, structural elements are exposed but never lacquered, echoing the effect of rusticity and airiness which harmonizes the interior and exterior space. Critics have suggested that the continual stressing of rusticity and creative innovation (*sakui*) of tea men sometimes itself borders on artifice. But in works such as this villa, it is clear that even when such effort is discernible it is directed away from showy confrontation and towards harmonious union.

External influences and the arts

The Ōnin wars (1467–77) ended Ashikaga power and the subsequent decades of civil strife saw the emergence of several dictator-warlords. During the same period, a new merchant class arose whose fortunes lay in brewing and money lending in Kyoto. This rising upper merchant class (*machishū*) and the increasingly impoverished aristocracy (*kuge*) shared the same political interests. The crude and often violent methods of the provincial military upstarts, for example, could hardly fail to provoke resistance among those who had hitherto enjoyed luxury and freedom. The aristocracy often depended on the *machishū* to bail them out of financial difficulties and the latter, through frequent contacts with the court, soon developed similar cultural preferences.

Nobunaga, who destroyed the Muromachi *bakufu* in 1573 and burnt down northern Kyoto as a reprisal for alleged insubordination, was assassinated in 1582 and his successor, Hideyoshi, took over control of foreign trade which had spawned Japanese mercantile colonies in Manila, Siam, and other ports of Southeast Asia. Hideyoshi exacted punishing levies to finance his disastrous Korean compaigns of 1592 and 1597. He died in 1598 and his remaining forces were vanquished by Tokugawa Ieyasu who instituted a central government in Edo (Tokyo). Ieyasu eventually gained complete control and subjected all potential rivals to severe regulations. The most effective of these was a system of hostages and attendance at the Shōgun's court in Edo, where the families of all the *daimyō* (provincial feudal lords) had to live, while the *daimyō* themselves spent alternate years in Edo and their own domains. In time the *daimyō* began to vie with each other for bigger and more splendid mansions in Edo; this rivalry kept their economic strength in check and stimulated a diverse and lively phase of artistic production in the new capital.

Contact with Europeans also affected Japanese culture at this time. By 1580 there were over 150,000 Christians in Japan and double that number fifty years later. European traders were quick to follow the Christian missionaries. Portuguese traders came to western Kyūshū by 1543 and were followed in 1593 by Spanish Franciscans. Protestant Dutch set up their trading post in Hirado in 1609 and were joined by the English in 1613. The Protestants convinced Ieyasu that foreign trade did not depend on missionaries, and that allegiance to God above all posed a potential threat. By 1617 the Christian faith was so strongly rooted that Ieyasu banned it on penalty of death. Tokugawa Iemitsu expelled the Spanish and the Portuguese and in 1636 decreed that no Japanese was to leave the country and no 'foreigners', not even the thousands of Japanese colonials then living abroad, were ever to set foot on Japanese soil. This left Japan's foreign trade to Chinese and Dutch ships, which were allowed to dock at Nagasaki and its small island of Dejima respectively. Despite this isolationist policy, foreign trade with China, Korea and Southeast Asia flourished. Korean trade was conducted by the Sō clan, lords of Tsūshima. The Chinese trade remained in the hands of Ming loyalists sailing from resistance centres in Fujian, and until the 1680s, decades after the Manchu conquest of China, the Tokugawa court held debates on the loyalists' request for military aid in arms and personnel.

However, once passion for western knowledge, or 'Dutch learning', had been fired it could not be extinguished. In spite of Japan's politically isolationist stand, European trade continued under Dutch auspices. Astronomy, medicine, the natural sciences and foreign languages were eagerly studied. In the arts, perspective drawing and life sketches of flora and fauna became permanently established. Oil painting, which began with the copying of Christian icons, was also practised. But the most attractive novelty for the Japanese painter was the depiction of 'Southern Barbarians' (*Namban*). The Europeans, with their curious, waisted garments and plumed head gear, their sharply chiselled features and curly hair, were portrayed with a keen eye for detail. Their enormous galleons were of special interest. European textile patterns, fabrics and colour schemes found their way into Japan; the bi-cultural ceramics of Furuta Oribe and his followers are particularly striking examples of artistic assimilation.

During Hideyoshi's Korean campaigns, the Way of Tea was fashionable and *daimyō* in western Japan quickly noticed the artless simplicity of

115 *Namban* (Southern Barbarians) screen. Part of six-fold screen; colours on paper, *c.* 1600.

Korean pottery and its suitability for the teahouse. Many Korean potters were invited, even abducted, by western lords to set up kilns in various parts of Kyūshū. This burst of artistic immigration led to a dramatic flowering of Japanese ceramics, resulting in influences which can still be seen today in Europe and North America.

The new tea fashions were also popular among the new middle class (*machishū*) in major manufacturing and commercial centres such as Sakai, Kyoto and Hakata. Fresh ceramic styles such as Shino, Oribe and Yellow Seto vied with the original Kamakura Seto wares, and kilns gradually shifted from Seto in Owari to Mino further west. The warm, cream-white-bodied Shino ware, usually covered with a rich feldspathic glaze, often with simple under-glaze designs in iron slip, is typical of the Momoyama period. Usually the rosy tone of the body glows from beneath the glaze. This heavily potted, thickly glazed ware is still highly regarded for the simplicity of its decoration and its sense of vulnerability and imperfection. The water-jar *Kōgan* (Ancient Shore) is hand-crafted in generous proportions and decorated to reflect the rural interests of native potters: three reeds and criss-cross grasses are swiftly but confidently

117

brushed on, and the bottom of the foot-rim is tooled with a sharp knife. It is prized for the cracks and glaze imperfections which enhance the feeling of distant antiquity and a sense of yearning. In another, later type of Shino ware, a grey-toned (*nezumi*) vessel was first covered with a high iron slip, parts of which were scraped off to reveal the white body. Then the rich Shino glaze was applied and the pot was fired in a reduction kiln which turned the underlying iron to a dark mouse-grey. 116

Bizen ware is rich, reddish-brown and unglazed. After the scratching and gouging, the potter allowed natural ash to drift over parts of the inverted 'old hag's mouth' and the cylindrical body. Asymmetrical ear-handle loops were added, and the indentation caused when removing the freshly potted vase from its wheel base was left uncorrected. These details, partly natural and partly devised for the much admired effect of creative ingenuity (*sakui*), were greatly prized by tea men.

Iga ware is thickly glazed with deep cracks and a rough texture. The Momoyama water-jar *Yabure bukuro* (Broken Pouch) is typical. The coarse clay contained quartz particles which made it difficult to handle on the wheel, so Iga wares were often hand-coiled. When it was fired, the 118

116 Small dish in *nezumi* Shino glaze Momoyama, 16th–17th century.

117 (*below left*) Kōgan (Ancient Shore) water-jar in Shinō ware. Momoyama, 16th–17th century.

118 (*below right*) Iga ware, *Yabure-Bukuro* (Torn Pouch), water-jar. Momoyama, 16th–17th century

quartz particles came to the surface and, with the flying wood ash swirling in the kiln, fused into a blue-grey glaze with scorched and greenish spots. In the late twentieth century it is easy to accept such pots as 'art objects'. Indeed, contemporary ceramic art around the world is still deeply influenced by Bernard Leach's discovery and emulation of Japanese folk pottery. With complete freedom, the Japanese folk potter prizes expression above technique. Through his wares, Western ceramists learned to break the geometric concept of form, and plane-oriented decoration – a major breakthrough in Western pottery design.

At the same time as Bizen and other major tea-ware kilns flourished, Korean artisans were introducing technical innovations such as the climbing kiln and high-fired porcelains. These lustrous, thin, white porcelains with under-glaze blue-line designs were shipped from the port of Imari, hence the generic name 'Imari ware'. In 1616, the Korean potter Ri Sampei eventually found white potting clay at Arita where he built his first linked-chamber climbing kiln. In Europe, Korean and Chinese porcelains were highly prized and were being imported in large quantities. The *daimyō* were naturally keen to reproduce such wares locally and many kilns for porcelain were built in the area. By the Genroku era (1688–1704) their continental style of decoration had been replaced by Japanese motifs.

In 1628 the official kiln of the Nabeshima domain was founded to raise standards and ensure clan control of the proceeds. In 1675 the kiln site was moved to Ōkōchiyama where the finest Nabeshima ware was produced. Plates, bowls, side-dishes and *sake* decanters were made. Their inner surfaces are finished in smooth curves and their decoration, often echoing lacquer designs, features the newly mastered technique of filling the underglaze blue outlines in bright overglaze colours of green and yellow, together with an unusually attractive and subdued beige-tinted red. Later, a lovely pale aubergine was added to the palette. The designs treat the entire surface as a continuous background unbroken by planes; overglaze enamels are carefully applied so as not to spill out beyond the underglaze outlines beneath. One of Japan's authorities on ceramics, Mikami Tsugio, complains of Nabeshima ware that 'beauty itself is subordinate to the all-important standard'. This is a typical Japanese observation, reflecting a preference for spontaneity and originality above technical perfection.

As Nabeshima wares flourished, so did their folk counterpart and predecessor in overglaze enamels, Old Imari, also in Arita. These are unabashedly decorated in bright primary colours, often with the addition of gilt. In the southern tip of Kyūshū the Satsuma kilns produced a buff ware with a fine-crackled glaze and distinctive, colourful decorations

119 Five small plates signed by Ōgata Kenzan. White slip and rust glaze, decorated with grey and gold pigment. Edo, early 18th century.

120 Nabeshima plate with design of flowering buckwheat. Overglaze enamels on porcelain. Early 19th century.

121 Old Imari *sake* bottle depicting Europeans. Edo, 17th century.

often marked with gold bosses. During the second half of the seventeenth century, when China was too embroiled in war for trade, the Dutch East India Company turned to Kyūshū and encouraged the export of Imari and Kakiemon wares, with their characteristic iron-red lip-rings, from the Arita area.

As well as in pots, Tokugawa foreign trade also dealt in lacquers and metalwork, often completely inlaid with intricate ivory or mother-of-pearl, in manners pleasing to the European eye. The Victoria and Albert Museum, London, for example, has a group of lacquered inlays, imported before the Hirado port was closed in 1623, which includes 122 bowls, chests and other items specifically made to western orders. Europeans enjoyed Japanese ceramics as much as Chinese wares, but developed a special fondness for Japanese lacquers, called *japon* in France. The interplay of influences between European and Japanese craftsmen can be seen in household furnishings and ceramics of this period.

158

122 Lacquered wooden chest with floral inlay of mother-of-pearl and gold foil on paper. Early 18th century. (See p. 169)

Art of the Machishū

By the early eighteenth century Japanese society was resigned to the Tokugawa hegemony. Although the nobility and upper merchant class had paid a heavy price in power and influence, it was nonetheless this class which, in the late sixteenth century, had launched the last and most glorious reincarnation of Japan's classical traditions.

Hon'ami Kōetsu (1558–1637) was from a distinguished family of sword connoisseurs well known among the wealthy patrician families in the imperial cultural circle. In 1615 Tokugawa Ieyasu, perhaps as a gesture of appeasement toward the *machishū*, granted Kōetsu a large tract of land in Takagamine, north-east of Kyoto. There Kōetsu established a colony of craftsmen of the Nichiren Buddhist school and inspired and directed the production of art works of unparalleled quality and diversity. Kōetsu had been educated in the Heian-oriented courtly arts and in the early fourteenth century Shōrenin style of royal calligraphy. He also studied the calligraphy style of the fourth-century Chinese aristocratic Wang Xizhi

159

123, 124 *Irises* by Ōgata Kōrin. Double six-fold screen; colours and gold foil on paper. Early 18th century. (See p. 169)

and was judged one of the finest calligraphers of his day. He brought his genius to bear on lacquer, painting, gardens, poetry, tea and ceramics: no form of art failed to benefit from his influence. He dazzled Kyoto society by publishing the tenth-century *Tale of Ise* and the twelfth-century *Hōjō-ki*, inscribed in his own elegant calligraphy on specially produced paper decorated with his own designs based on Heian ideals. He also published song-books from the Nō theatre: this too focussed cultural attention on the past.

Kōetsu's colony included not only artists but also paper-makers, lacquerers and brush-makers. These craftsmen, inspired by Kōetsu's guiding spirit, collaborated with the artists and with each other to produce works of a standard unmatched since Heian times. A fine

125 example is the writing box called *Boat Bridge*, which contains inkstone, ink and brush. It is clearly inspired by Heian lacquers such as the twelfth

126 century *Waves and Wheel of Life*, with its gold and mother-of-pearl inlaid wave design interspersed with a wheel motif. Kōetsu added the common base metal, lead, to gold and silver – a striking innovation – laying it across the convex top and the sides in the form of a bridge, floating on gold lacquer supporting boats in low relief. Although the box is nearly square, the decoration is entirely asymmetrical. Three boats bob up and down out of phase; the tiny raised-line waves lap in yet another rhythm and the bridge, which gives the box its name, is wrapped around the entire work at an angle. Balance is restored by Kōetsu's inscription of a *waka* poem, applied in high relief in silver over the whole scene.

125 *Boat Bridge*, writing-box by Hon'ami Kōetsu. Inkstone case, lead and mother-of-pearl on gold lacquer. Early 17th century.

126 *Waves and Wheel of Life.* Lacquer handbox; gold and mother-of-pearl inlay. Heian, 12th century.

127 *Fujisan, raku* ware tea-bowl by Kōetsu. Momoyama, early 17th century.

128 *Kuro Oribe chawan*, tea-bowl by Furuta Oribe. Momoyama, 16th–17th century.

A man of tea, Kōetsu made many tea bowls. In *Fujisan*, doubtless by his own hand, he created the most superb Japanese *raku* tea bowl of all time. It has taut, straight sides tapering slightly towards the bottom. The reddish body is covered entirely in a blackish matt slip with opaque white glaze over the upper half, leaving the darker glaze for the bottom: the effect produced by firing is that of gently falling snow. The vigour and grandeur of Mont Fuji are suggested. There is nothing of the cleverness or cuteness which are so often the downfall of tea bowl makers with too much zest for *sakui*. The impression is of monumentality. In tea ware such as this, Kōetsu echoed the simplicity and purity of Rikyū's time, following the forthright form produced by Chōjirō. His work was in stark contrast to that of his contemporary, Furuta Oribe (1543–1615) who had achieved a lively and remarkable synthesis of free-form *raku* ceramic style and Western patterns and colouring.

Kōetsu collaborated with the sensitive and skilled painter Sōtatsu (who never joined the Takagamine artistic colony but worked out of his Kyoto establishment which sold decorated paper and painted fans to the *machishū* and aristocracy). Sōtatsu produced beautiful designs for Kōetsu's calligraphy paper in long handscrolls, fan shapes and square board *shikishi*. He applied them in silver and gold by hand and by woodblock impressions. Both masters were inspired by Heian *waka* inscriptions on decorated paper. In the example shown here, Sōtatsu, with a brush dipped alternately in gold and silver, has painted flowers and grasses of the four seasons in sequence. The ancient Chinese method of 'boneless' painting'

129 *Flowers and Grasses of the Four Seasons* by Kōetsu (calligraphy) and Sōtatsu (painting). Detail of handscroll. Momoyama, early 17th century.

(without ink outlines) was given a new sense of liveliness by Sōtatsu who combined it with a pooling device called *tarashikomi*. This Japanese method of dropping ink or colour pigment on to still-wet areas of the paper or silk may well have been invented by Sōtatsu. Here the silver flowers and golden leaves appear in different intensities, seeming to emerge from dense mists.

Kōetsu's calligraphy equally reflects classical preferences. Even on relatively unabsorbent paper he fully controls every stroke and dot. The inclusion of cursive Chinese characters among the *kana* syllabary echoes the effect of leaves and flowers among stems. Kōetsu alternates between thick and thin, large and small strokes but the wrist pressure is steady, changing with the column rather than within single letter or word configurations. Kōetsu's calligraphy is more stately than Heian proto-types, carrying traces of the China-inspired symmetry of the Muromachi period, and producing a synthesis of the two styles.

130 *Flowers and Grasses* by Kōrin. Handscroll; colours and white pigment on paper. c. 1705. (See p. 169)

うくさきの
松と三毛来
おか13

131 *Pine Tree at Karasaki* by Yosa Buson. Detail from handscroll. 1778. (See p. 175)

Sōtatsu's association with Kōetsu and *machishū* collectors, with their nostalgia for the art of the past, and his own contact with the finest Heian traditions in painting when he restored the *Heike nōgyō* and other masterworks, led him to create a new world of poetic imagery in an energetic revival and reinvigoration of Heian motifs. His school came to be known as *Rimpa*. (This style has often mistakenly been called decorative. If 'decorative' means 'serving to decorate' or 'purely ornamental', then we must say that there is hardly anything decorative in Japanese art at all, at least since Shōsōin days. Japanese artists seem incapable of static, purely visual, patternistic decoration. Be it lyrical, contemplative, dramatic or aggressive, nearly all Japanese art is united in one essence: emotion. It may be more appropriate to call the *Rimpa* style evocative.)

Everything Sōtatsu created, whether fan and screen paintings, underpaintings for Kōetsu or his own ink monochrome works, such as the *Oxen* in the Chōmyōji in Kyoto, combines visual beauty with considerable emotional intensity. Vignettes taken from Chinese woodblock

65

printed books are radically transformed and japanized. The elements in *Lotus and Swimming Birds* are so placed as to share the space, not to divide it. The forms are not self-contained and permanent, each commanding its sphere; rather, they depend on and interact with each other. The psychological energy typical of Japanese forms is mostly turned outward. The use of watery ink in pooled *tarashikomi*, especially on the leaves, gives a sense of expansion and, as in the 'emotive cloud' device, creates an emotional quickening analogous to a blush or the sound of breathing. But the ebullience of the Momoyama period marks the works of Kōetsu and Sōtatsu with energy and immediacy, in contrast to the dreaminess of their Heian models.

About half a century after Kōetsu and Sōtatsu, the Ōgata brothers Kōrin (1658–1716) and Kenzan (1663–1743) consolidated the *Rimpa* style. Their father had been a member of Kōetsu's artistic community and transmitted its spirit to his sons. Kenzan, the younger brother, was a calligrapher and ceramicist. He studied first with Ninsei, then with Kōetsu's grandson, Kūchū, and became a celebrated potter, combining the dignity and nobility of Kōetsu with the inventiveness of Oribe. A Zen Buddhist in his late twenties and thirties, Kenzan felt that beauty of things was seen as such, and had no place for *mono-no-aware* or other associative sentiments. His brushwork is weighty and disciplined, his style compelling and reserved.

If Kenzan was introvert, Kōrin was a determined extrovert. The two brothers lived in the boisterous Genroku period (1688–1704) which saw the eclipse of the *machishū* elite by the lower merchant classes (*chōnin*) and Kōrin entered drunkenly, sardonically into the spirit of the times. Once at

132

119,133

132 (*opposite*) *Lotus and Swimming Birds* by Sōtatsu. Hanging scroll; ink on paper. Momoyama, early 17th century.

133 *Waterfall* tea-bowl by Kenzan. White slip glaze and rust painting. Early 18th century.

134 *Fruit* by Kobayashi Kokei. Hanging scroll; mineral pigments on paper. Early 20th century. (See p. 193)

135 *Stream* by Tokuoka Shinsen. Colours on paper. 1954. (See p. 196)

a picnic, while the bourgeois displayed their elaborately lacquered gold and silver picnic boxes, Kōrin astounded them by unwrapping his food from plain bamboo leaves which turned out to be gold-foiled on the inside and which he proceeded to toss casually into the river. On another occasion, he engineered a beauty contest so that the winner was a beautiful woman plainly dressed in white with a black wrapper, while her attendant wore sumptuous colours.

Kōrin's work, in textile and lacquer design as well as in painting, was notable for its urbane elegance. It is less a nostalgic recreation of Heian style than a deliberate display of virtuosity. Typical of his work at its flamboyant best are the *Red and White Prunus* screens in the Atami Museum, the *Waves* screens at the Metropolitan Museum, New York, and his copy of Sōtatsu's *Thunder and Lightning Gods*. In *Irises* he boldly covers a double six-fold screen with brilliant repetitions of a single motif: blue irises, green leaves. The four groups on the right, in inverted triangle formation, gently descend, while five unequal groups on the left-hand screen increase in size and height towards the left. The rest is gold-foil. There are no plank-bridges, rippling waves, meandering earthen banks or emotive clouds: the work is hard-edged and uncompromising. Motion is created in the asymmetrical grouping and the out-of-phase repetition of the motif. It is here and in his daring and unrelenting use of gold, blue and green that Kōrin displays his supreme self-confidence. Since Heian times, irises had been associated with the eight-fold plank bridge, *yatsu hashi*, zig-zagging over swamps, among wild flowers. In the Heian *Tale of Ise* the hero pauses by a stream banked with wild irises. Kōrin removed the bridge and the hero, reducing the image to the flowers alone. As Sōtatsu had turned his viewer into an aerobatic sea bird, so Kōrin turned him into the hero of the *Ise* tale, enchanted mid-bridge. By removing all external props, 'framework' or 'borders', both men plunge the viewer into the scene, and create a sense of immediacy and personal involvement.

Throughout his work, Kōrin took the asymmetry of Kōetsu and Sōtatsu to exaggerated extremes. His lacquer inkstone box, for example, uses gold, silver, mother-of-pearl and pewter in another reworking of the *yatsu hashi* bridge-and-iris theme. The bridge is inlaid with lead like Kōetsu's but the angle is much steeper. Similarly, in studies of flying cranes, Kōrin's fly upwards at a much sharper angle than those of Kōetsu or Sōtatsu. This tendency to sharpen the angle and to tilt the ground up towards the vertical plane, also present in Kōrin's landscapes, is particularly dramatic in his *Red and White Prunus*.

Kōrin's watercolour sketches are quite distinct from the stylish glitter of his other works. *Flowers and Grasses* for example, which probably dates

123,124

136

130

136 Inkstone box with *yatsu hashi* (eight-fold plank bridge); designed by Kōrin. Edo, 18th century.

from 1705 when he first went to live in Edo, is relaxed and intimate. Working in a 'boneless' technique, he outlines the blue and white flower petals in a fluid, evocative calligraphic style and the leaves and smaller flowers are borderless and further softened by the use of *tarashikomi*.

Textiles

By the middle of the seventeenth century Japan's own silk industry flourished, bringing an end to reliance on Chinese imports. In textiles, as in all Japanese tactile arts created for the private, not public domain (floor, wall and ceiling surfaces, ceramics), native preferences dominated. The richness of fabric production and variety of design proclaim a time of peace and prosperity.

The creation and decoration of Japanese garments, like ceramics, were conceived as a single artistic activity and the design was integral to the garment. Clothes, with long or short but always broad sleeves, were created in designs of stunning daring, seldom matched even in Paris fashion houses. A robe spread on a lacquer hanger might well be used as a room-divider, like an evocative screen. Geometric waves and birds on a black ground or a diagonal grouping of wisteria and chrysanthemum on a white ground are typical patterns.

Momoyama and Edo artisans were masters of several techniques which included dyeing, embroidery, brocade, appliquée, raised gold-thread repoussé and hand-painting. The demand for innovation in textiles was insatiable, not only in Nō theatre and noble houses but also among the wealthy *machishū* and *chōnin*. This example is from a shōgunal household and shows the sophistication of these techniques; embroidery has been

137

used to accent the flower-and-leaf shapes already created in the dyeing process and the peacock ground and feather loops made with gold repoussé. Another striking robe, made for a courtesan, uses gold-foil for dramatic effect. It features a hawk and a dragon in action and is made of velvet, a European fabric, whose novelty coupled with the remarkable design must have achieved the desired startling effect. 138

Humbler folk wore cottons and, occasionally, silks. They enjoyed a variety of designs with largely Southeast Asian (rather than continental) sources. The ancient technique of *ikat* was often used to create bold designs. Cotton yarn was tied in sections and dyed indigo; the result was an alternation of white and indigo in the weaving. Warp or weft yarns, or both, could be partially dyed in this way. Warp-*ikat* fabrics are the most common; weft-*ikat* is rarer and double-*ikat*, the most difficult to make, is

137 Detail of peacock on *kosode* (short-sleeved robe). Gold thread repoussée and embroidery. Edo.

138 *Hawk and Dragon*, courtesan's *kosode*. Gold on black velvet. Edo, early 19th century.

139 *Rooster and Flowering Tree*, cotton panel, originally a bedcover. Resist-dyed on an indigo ground and mounted as a double screen. Meiji, late 19th century.

139 rarer still. All three methods were common in Japan during the Edo period, and were called *kasuri*. Another technique with Southeast Asian origins is *batik* (resist-dye) which, using only dark and light indigo on white, nevertheless provided a great variety of designs for peasant wear. Humbler still are the banded and striped fabrics which combine cotton yarns of different colours in a straight weave. Home dyers also used a paste-resist method which seems to have been derived from twelfth-century China. A mixture of boiled, glutinous rice and rice bran was applied through a tube or poured or stencilled on to the cloth, which was then dyed. The process could be repeated with several colours, giving a splendid polychrome effect. The Art Gallery of Greater Victoria in British Columbia, Canada, has some handsome examples of this folk art; clearly, a strong awareness of beauty and design was present in Japanese society at every level.

Nanga *(Idealist painting)*

In an effort to promote loyalty towards themselves, the Tokugawa shōgunate established Confucian centres of learning and produced a new class of esteemed but powerless Confucianists. The 250-year spread of Chinese learning, however, resulted in some unexpected turns of thought. Foremost was the notion that loyalty was owed to the Emperor, not to his military spokesman; this, together with a growing awareness of the outside world, eventually led to the overthrow of the *bakufu* and restoration of imperial authority in 1868. Meanwhile, China's contagious love of its own past created something like an identity crisis among Japanese sinophiles. They found themselves yearning for what they had come to regard as the source of their civilization: ancient China. In painting, the ideal of the Chinese scholar-amateur-painter was introduced and the Japanese were appalled to discover they had been following the lesser tradition, and that Japan had missed the true essence of Chinese painting by pursuing the styles of Southern Song and Ming academies rather than the free expression of lofty ideals represented in the *wenren* painting of Chinese scholar-amateurs.

In China, idealist painting was enjoyed by the leisured class as an activity of taste and cultivation. Originally such paintings incorporated poetry written in superb calligraphy and the works were meant for the private enjoyment of small groups of highly cultivated associates. Japan lacked a scholar-bureaucrat class, and idealist painting became an avenue for departure from traditions of various kinds: it was taken up by discontented members of the *samurai* class, by the new breed of scholars, by monks, physicians, merchants and professional painters. Late Ming Chinese texts called idealist painting *Nanzong-hua* (Southern School Painting); in Japan it was called *Nanga* (Southern painting) but was strictly for sale. Geographical and technical features distinguish the Northern Academy (rocky peaks, angular brushwork) from the Southern Amateur (rounded hills; long, rope-like brush-strokes) traditions in China; in Japan, the Shūbun school had worked mostly in Northern styles, while Sōami's works were often of Southern origin. But this was clearly not understood by Sōami or early Tokugawa theorists, and the distinction between the two schools was not fully appreciated till the end of the eighteenth century.

The first experiments of Japanese painters in the new mode produced some curious results drawn largely from a mixture of contemporary Chinese provincial imports. The Mampukuji monastery outside Kyoto, founded in 1661 under Tokugawa patronage, became the very centre of Chinese culture in Japan, and its (largely Fujianese) clergy were permitted Chinese imports and totally Chinese lifestyles. Their artistic and other imports from strife-ridden China were avidly sought after by Japanese fanciers without regard to quality or stylistic origins. The professional

満廳潮陰迴気
先衡
霞雅寫件題

140 *Pine Tree and Waves* by Ikeno Taiga. One of a double six-fold screen; light colours on paper. *c.* 1765–70.

painter Sakaki Hyakusen (1698–1753), however, drew upon works of higher calibre from late Ming Suzhou. Ikeno Taiga (1723–1776) boldly and radically transformed his models, even though his contact with Chinese paintings and Japanese collectors was limited largely to the Mampukuji circle, as he did not have the access to the imperial and shōgunal treasuries granted to orthodox painters like Kanō Tanyū. On the other hand, running his own fan shop in Kyoto gave him independence from particularized patronage, and more artistic freedom than Tanyū. Tanyū's study of Chinese paintings was academic: precise line copies of ancient masterpieces in shōgunal and other collections. Taiga interpolated, mixed and invented, and even produced manual-scrolls of Southern School methods, playfully attributing Chinese names without real basis. *Pine Tree and Waves*, done in his forties, displays a thoroughly Japanese use of ink and brush, and transforms what had been a rather stiff provincial Fujian manner into a comfortable picture of an ancient tree at ease. The rendering is abbreviated, with only traces of the Fujian models available to him in Mampukuji (with notable circular bark strokes) and harmonizes perfectly with waves done in traditional Japanese style. By the time of this painting, Taiga had confidently absorbed and transformed diverse traditions, but his own vision speaks above them all. The mediocrity of his models was immaterial, as he selected only compositional motifs and technical innovations which interested him.

Taiga transformed the sedate and introspective Chinese scholar-amateur tradition into something thoroughly extrovert, endowing the genre with luminosity and lyricism. A host of pupils and followers carried his vision forwards and made of *nanga* a viable tradition. The celebrated *haiku* poet Yosa Buson (1716–83), who enlivened his verse inscriptions with whimsical *haiga* illustrations, also painted in the newly fashionable manner. His *Pine Tree at Karasaki* was painted in 1778, two years after Taiga's death. The giant, ancient pine, resting on wooden supports, dwarfs the small house. The brush is charged with wet colour wash to such an extent that the image seems flooded with unreal light, as if alluding to some unstated past. In contrast, Buson's calligraphy is crisp, fluid and assured, speaking of the present.

The *samurai* Uragami Gyokudō (1745–1820) served the branch of the Ikeda family until 1794 when, despondent over his wife's death and generally disillusioned, he resigned his post to take up *nanga* painting. His style is notable for its highly personal brushwork. James Cahill points out a resemblance to seventeenth-century Chinese painters who overlaid dry brush-strokes over wet, light strokes over dark, creating a tapestry effect. A critical and profound difference is that Gyokudō applied the stroke series in layers. Thus, a layer of horizontal modelling strokes might be

141
131

141 *Sumō Wrestling* by Yosa Buson. Hanging scroll; ink, light colours on paper, inscribed with *haiku* verses by Buson. Mid-18th century. (See also pl. 131)

142 *High Winds and Banking Geese* by Uragami Gyokudō. Album leaf; ink and light colours on paper. 1817.

143 (*opposite*) *Birthday Felicitations* by Aoki Mokubei. Hanging scroll; ink and light colours on satin. 1830.

covered in turn by a layer of cross-hatching, a layer of wet dots, and a layer of dry black-ink scratches. The result is that what had been depicted in Chinese paintings in depth, the strokes intertwining as in a nest and built up perpendicularly to the painting surface, was in its Japanese transformation re-ordered along the picture plane, creating lateral tension between the elements; the method, often mis-identified as merely decorative, in fact achieves the visual clarity and luminosity beloved in Japan. A fine example is *High Winds and Banking Geese*, a work from Gyokudō's seventy-third year. Archaic Chinese script, rendered with deliberate awkwardness, contrasts with the explosive energy of the swirling, cyclone-like brush-work. All motion is circular: even mountains are reshaped into cylinders and rounded rocks. The geese and the fishing-boats are incidental; the subject of the picture is energy, direct, raw and exhilarating: being alive.

Among the most original *nanga* masters is the painter and potter Aoki Mokubei (1767–1833) whose works in diverse media are marked with dynamic inner cohesion and a strong sense of inter-relatedness, both among the pictorial elements and between work and viewer. In *Birthday Felicitations* (1830), he celebrates a friend's seventieth birthday in a scene aglow with serenity and wellbeing. Painted on satin, the swirling mists (done in dry ink lines) suggest a cipher for a dragon, providing the gravity and mystery proper to the occasion. Psychological energy converges towards the centre (and the viewer), from the craggy pine of longevity on the right and from the left from the God of Longevity himself as he ambles towards the centre, followed by his child attendant with the parasol of state. The focal point is the confluence of clouds, tree energy and long life beneath the mountain peak (placed left of centre to balance with the inscription on the upper right).

Diversification of schools

The long peace brought wealth, and its wider distribution brought more patrons, and more art. In Kyoto alone, besides the traditional styles of Kanō and *Rimpa* and the newly-established *nanga*, yet another style appeared and was soon to dominate. Maruyama Ōkyō (1733–95) had studied with Kanō masters and then became interested in Western perspective and Chinese painting: his style was a synthesis of all three traditions. Not the least of his activities was to paint Japanese scenes for the newly-imported Chinese viewing-device, where a picture was reflected and magnified. In China, Suzhou artists had been producing

144 *Sketches of Cicadas* (detail) by Maruyama Ōkyō, from his *Sketchbook of Insects*. Ink and light colours on paper. Mid-19th century.

145 *The Itsukushima Shrine*, fifth view of *Eight Views of Miyajima* (Hiroshima) by Nagasawa Rosetsu. Album leaf; ink and colours on silk. 1794.

woodblock prints with Western perspectives for such viewing boxes; Ōkyō supplied the demand for new and Japanese views. He also produced scrolls and large screens, combining a gold ground with majestic pines, or peacocks on rocks in the Chinese academic style, or wisteria in Japanese-style colour wash. He investigated, in short, every available style, format and subject. He taught his pupils to sketch directly from nature, and

144 produced some of his own most charming works in this genre.

Ōkyō was enthusiastically supported by a former pupil of Buson, Matsumura Goshun (1752–1811) and their combination of talents came to be known as the Maruyama-Shijō school. For a while it was lively and active but in the nineteenth century it quickly declined into saccharine sentimentality.

The most individual of Ōkyō's pupils, Nagasawa Rōsetsu (1754–99), possessed a vision which is as fresh and vital today as it must have seemed to his contemporaries. From a warrior family, he changed his name in order to paint rather than be subject to official positions. His first works were in the manner of Ōkyō, but after mastering Western techniques of perspective and *chiaroscuro*, he began to contribute to the eccentric and grotesque modes then fashionable. He worked in ink wash as well as in fine lines and colours, on silk and paper, painting everything from fans to murals. In four to five months in 1786, travelling through Kii, Rosetsu painted no less than 180 wall-panels and sliding doors for four separate monasteries. The *Itsukushima Shrine* from Rosetsu's *Eight Views of Miyajima* (1794) is a bird's-eye view rendered deftly in ink, sometimes very fine and dry, sometimes wet and diffused. The twisting covered walk and the main hall (with its stage-like front for performing sacred dances) both rise on stilts from the water. It is twilight, and stone-and-paper lanterns have been lit to dispel the misty gloom, descending upon the pine-clad isle. 145

Another great individualist was Itō Jakuchū (1716–1800). His works are in colours and ink monochrome and show barnyard fowl, vegetables, flowers and trees in elegant distortion. He combined foreshortening and perspective techniques with a flat, highly chromatic use of ink and brilliant colours. He turned his animal paintings into still-lifes with a sharp wit, posturing the figures in an exaggerated manner, comically suggesting human behaviour. His strutting male and submissive female birds, for example, strike poses reminiscent of *ukiyo-e* actor prints. Jakuchū was influenced by several schools: the Chinese Zhejiang style of

Shen Nanping (which became in Japan the Nagasaki school) introduced in the 1730s, the late Ming Fujianese Ōbaku (Mampukuji) techniques of Chen Xian, Japanese Kanō gold screen decoration, as well as the Western ideas mentioned above. The peculiar use of a very wet brush charged with pale ink in a rapid series of parallel strokes to form textured surfaces such as dragons, feathers and the like, suggests familiarity with the 'trance' folk-painting of religious festivals. He also originated a most bizarre and laborious painting technique. A double six-fold screen features a phoenix and an enormous white elephant each surrounded by outlandish birds and animals. In this astonishing composition Jakuchū imitates in paint mosaic, certain effects of Indian calico cloth, or Qing paintings on woven paper strips forming tiny squares. Each screen was underpainted with 310 vertical and 140 horizontal lines making approximately 43,000 squares each measuring 1.2 cm. After the paper was primed with white, each

146 *Phoenix and White Elephant* by Itō Jakuchū. One of a pair of six-fold screens. Ink and colour *impasto* on paper. Mid-18th century.

square was separately filled with colour. In the centre of each square was a smaller area of the same or lighter tone. This extraordinary style had no imitators; the few works which survive all originate from Jakūchū himself or his atelier.

Although Edo (Tokyo) was a new, upstart city compared with Kyoto (Heian), the shōgunal presence drew many talents there; there was a proliferation of artistic schools working for the *daimyō*, and it was a centre for Chinese and Western ('Dutch') learning. The Edo master Tani Bunchō (1763–1840) had a typically eclectic style: often counted among *Nanga* painters, he had also studied Kanō, Tosa, Nagasaki, *ukiyo-e* and

147 *Frog and Snail* by Gibon Sengai. Hanging scroll; ink on paper. Early 19th century.

Western techniques. Born into an established *samurai* family, Bunchō (unlike his fellow *Nanga* painters, who often represented anti-establishment sentiments) moved in prominent political circles. He wrote treatises on painting, and produced a series of woodblock prints featuring famous mountains. In the later years of his life he developed his well-known spontaneous, abbreviated style.

Always the clergy were enthusiastic calligraphers and painters. The Zen master Gibon Sengai (1750–1837) was the abbot of Shōfukuji in Hakata from 1790 until his retirement in 1811. His painting was in a simple, direct and spontaneous style; it was widely appreciated, and thought particularly 147 appropriate to the world of Tea. His characteristic *Frog and Snail* was done in a few rapid strokes with the brush only half-charged with wet ink. This results in unevenly inked line-edges, in both the calligraphy and the subject. The seven Chinese characters blend perfectly into the picture. Their meaning, 'Swallow the Three Buddhas, Past, Present and Future, in One Mouthful,' refers to the innate perfection of all: of frog, of snail, of swallowing. The lowly status but sacred potential of the frog was a common Buddhist theme.

The Zen master Hakuin Ekaku (1685–1768), who more than anyone revitalized and japanized Zen, expressed himself in a particularly bold and 149 powerful style. In a large portrait of Daruma (222.8 by 36.5 cms), he used his brush with such vehemence that the tip splayed in places, producing a dramatically rough-edged effect. Another Zen artist of this time, the 148 sculptor-monk Enkū (1628–95), wandered round the country and left many statues of Buddha and bodhisattvas in rough-hewn wood for peasants worshipping at regional Buddhist temples and Shintō shrines.

182

148 *(left) Shō Kannon Bosatsu* by Enkū. Unpainted
wood. Late 17th century.

149 *(above) Daruma* (Bodhidharma) by Hakuin
Ekaku. Hanging scroll; ink on paper. 1751.

183

Genre painting and the woodblock print

In the Edo period, diversity and elegance in the fine arts was easily matched by the robust humour and virile self-confidence of the rising lower mercantile class. Anonymous craftsmen working on everyday items such as ceramics, textiles, farm implements, architecture, household furnishings, book illustration and printing catered for mass tastes. For ordinary people, peasants and townsmen alike, this was a vigorous artistic period. And it is this new urban culture which marks the most notable departure from previous eras. Although the Tokugawa had placed merchants beneath farmers and artisans in the new social hierarchy, this enterprising class nevertheless came increasingly to dominate Tokugawa life. In cities and in towns, they created a vigorous commercial economy: during this period Kyoto finally regained its importance as a centre for fine silks and ceramics. Enormously wealthy families (such as the Mitsui, who by the early twentieth century controlled the largest financial empire in the world) flourished; mass literacy was among the highest in the world; popular and satirical novels were extremely fashionable, and the printing business flourished.

Since the early sixteenth century a favourite art-form among the rising bourgeoisie had been genre-painting. These works featured a variety of popular recreations and amusements. Some showed elegant, beautiful 151 women in leisurely pursuits; they meticulously recorded details of dress. Later forms featured the more down-market activities of low grade prostitutes or bath-house attendants. One particularly popular type depicted entire city blocks and included street dancing, festival floats and interiors and exteriors of every kind. Scenes such as the anonymous *Shijō-* 150 *Kawara* are the apotheosis of bourgeois collective (if edited) self-portraiture. Towards the end of the seventeenth century, as the appeal of this kind of art increased, it began to be mass-produced. Urban life seemed at its most elegant and extravagant in the demi-monde of Edo, Kyoto, and Osaka: here, as the late Sir George Sansom put it, was 'the world of fugitive pleasures, of theatres and restaurants, wrestling booths and houses of assignation, with their permanent population of actors,

150 (*opposite*) *Shijō-Kawara*, one of a pair of bi-fold screens by an anonymous artist. Colours on gold paper. Early 17th century.

151 *Dancing under the Cherry Trees* by Kanō Naganobu. Detail from double six-fold screen; colours on paper. Early 17th century.

singers, story-tellers, jesters, courtesans, bathgirls and itinerant purvey-
ors, among whom mixed the profligate sons of rich merchants, dissolute
samurai and naughty apprentices'. The Japanese themselves confessed:

Living only for the moment, turning our full attention to the pleasures of
the moon, sun, the cherry blossoms and the maple leaves, singing songs,
drinking wine, and diverting ourselves just in floating, floating, caring
not a whit for the pauperism staring us in the face, refusing to be
disheartened, like a gourd floating along with the river current: this is
what we call *the floating world* (*ukiyo*) (from Asai Ryōi, trans. Richard
Lane, Tales of the Floating World).

This 'floating world' formed the prime subject matter both of genre
paintings and of the (now world-famous) Japanese woodblock prints.

Printed illustrations had been known in Buddhist circles since the Heian
period, but with the Edo boom in communications, the printed book
became an independent art-form. The literate bourgeoisie was hungry for
printed literature of the outspoken type which had long been part of the
vernacular tradition. Illustrations, particularly to bawdy tales, were in
great demand and astute publishers accordingly commissioned and
produced some of the world's most frank and joyous celebrations of
earthy pleasures. Equally, the spread of scientific interest and knowledge
resulted in the publication of medical and botanical books containing
exquisite drawings of plants and herbs. It was during this time that the
woodblock-carver's art soared to unexcelled heights.

In Edo, Hishikawa Moronobu and others began to produce black and
white prints, hand-coloured in orange-red. Many of these were overtly
and extravagantly erotic, and their style imitated the calligraphic character
of the ink-brushed line. By the early eighteenth century, a wider range of
colours, including an attractive rose-red and a deep-toned black resembling lacquer, was added. A great many hand-coloured actor-prints of
this type were produced in the early eighteenth century. In about 1745, a
more elaborate and expensive technique of multiblock colour printing
(probably learned from China) was used to produce limited editions of
calendar prints. Here, since each colour required a separate block,
meticulous accuracy in positioning the blocks was achieved by the use of
guide marks (*kentō*). Prints of this kind, large or small, were often
commissioned by a patron for distribution among friends.

The 'brocade prints' (*nishiki-e*) of Suzuki Harunobu (*fl.* 1765–70) were
the first to perfect the new and more costly techniques. In *Viewing Maple
Leaves by the Waterfall* a tipsy roué, kimono in disarray, holds a fan
inscribed with a line of poetry. He is oblivious to all but his nearer
companion who is holding him up by his belt, while the other woman

152

152 *Viewing Maple Leaves by the Waterfall* by Suzuki Harunobu. 'Brocade print' (*chūban nishiki-e*). Mid-18th century.

(both are courtesans) carries his outer garment. The waterfall in the background is in very fine lines, white and pink on grey; the man's face and arms are flushed with wine, in contrast to the white of the girls' faces. The beautiful garments, in pink, orange and lilac, show the fashions of the time. Harunobu uses an embossing technique to raise certain areas of the kimonos of the courtesans; by adding glue to the black, he achieves the intensity of lacquer in the man's garment. Compared with later prints, Harunobu's work is notable for its qualities of tenderness and innocence.

Later print-masters, like Kiyonaga, extolled the statuesque elegance of courtesans, highlighting their role as leaders of high fashion; Kitagawa Utamaro (1754–1806) produced many series showing women at home and in the 'licensed quarters'. *The Coquettish Type*, taken from a series 153 published about 1801–3, shows a close-up view of a woman just out of the bath; although her hair is meticulously piled up, her kimono is carelessly worn and the sash is loosely tied. The background has been rubbed with mica to produce a silvery grey, which highlights the warmth

153 *The Coquettish Type* by Kitagawa Utamaro, from the series *Ten Physiognomic Types of Women*. Polychrome wood-block print. Late 18th century.

154 *Sakata Hangorō III as the Villain Mizuyemon* by Sharaku. Polychrome woodblock print with mica-dusted background. 1794.

and softness of the fleshtones. Utamaro's prints, spicy, sardonic and psychologically acute, are among the most treasured by Western collectors and connoisseurs. His sensuous line, luxuriant colour and dynamic design influenced the work of painters like Toulouse-Lautrec.

The actor-prints featured the matinée idols of the time, the Kabuki actors. Prints announcing or celebrating particular performances, or portraying an actor in a certain role, functioned like movie-star posters today. Here was a medium for theatrical panache and irony. Eerie satire is the realm of Sharaku (*fl.* 1794–5). He may have been a Nō actor; certainly his hardly flattering view of the more popular Kabuki style seems to have offended Kabuki actors, and his publisher dropped him after only ten brilliant months. In his portrait of Sakata Hangorō III as the villain Mizuyemon, the squinting eyes, twisted mouth and contorted arms of the

154

155 *View on a Fine Breezy Day* by Katsushika Hokusai, from *Thirty-Six Views of Mount Fuji*. Polychrome wood-block print. 1822–32.

figure, set against the ominous, mica-flecked background, show how the designer can convey a sense of the drama by distortion. In fact at this period figurative prints, including those of actors, became increasingly grotesque; the phenomenon is also apparent in the paintings of Rosetsu, Jakuchū and others.

Little of this baroque exaggeration is found in the work of Katsushika Hokusai (1760–1849) whose fame grew out of his numerous cartoons (*manga*) or humorous sketches. His landscape prints discovered vigorous new life in an ancient form. He was the Sesshū of his day, drawing on a dazzling variety of sources, and fired by extraordinary creative energy; as he himself noted:

From the age of six I have had a mania for sketching the forms of things. From about the age of fifty I produced a number of designs, yet of all I drew prior to the age of seventy there is truly nothing of any great note. At the age of seventy-three I finally came to understand somewhat the nature of birds, animals, insects, fishes – the vital nature of grasses and

156 *Snow at Kambara* by Andō Hiroshige, from *Fifty-Three Stations of the Tōkaidō*. Polychrome wood-block print. 1833.

trees. Therefore at eighty I shall have made great progress, at ninety I shall have penetrated even further the deeper meaning of things, and at one hundred I shall have become truly marvellous, and at one hundred and ten, each dot, each line shall surely possess a life of its own.

(trans. Richard Lane)

155   His famous views of Mount Fuji, so overexposed as to seem banal, remain nevertheless a synthesis of supreme draftsmanship tinged with a remarkably humane view of the world he knows.

Encouraged by Hokusai's example, Andō Hiroshige (1797–1858) perfected a new genre of travelogue prints, with numerous series such as
156   *The Fifty-Three Stages of the Tōkaidō Highway.* Although he was less dynamic or gifted than Hokusai, he provided a more lyrical vision in which the poetry of mood is given often memorable expression, as here in the feeling of loneliness and quietude in the snow-covered pass at Kambara.

CHAPTER SEVEN

Modern Japan (1868–   )

By the middle of the nineteenth century the conservative and isolationist policies of the Tokugawa *bakufu* had been rendered untenable by several forces: the Confucian notion that the Emperor (Son of Heaven) was the only legitimate source of rule, the presence of Western gunboats demanding trade relations and a growing feeling among the intelligentsia that Japan was socially, politically and militarily backward among the world's nations. With the Meiji restoration in 1867, the Japanese made westernization and modernization their goals.

The cultural experience of the Meiji, Taishō and Shōwa eras included a massive ingestion of European and American learning. Japanese students studied in the West and foreigners established universities and colleges in Japan. The young Meiji Emperor and Empress were photographed in Western dress. Architecture aped British-Victorian grandeur. Western oil painting was called *Yōga* and students in Europe for long periods were able to effect japanization of its themes and techniques far more rapidly than in the Tokugawa period when foreign travel was banned. A good example of this is Kuroda Seiki (1866–1924) whose 1897 *Yōga* painting (in oils on canvas), *Lake Shore*, shows a woman resting by a lake after 157 bathing. Kuroda studied painting for nine years in Paris before returning to Japan in 1893 to open his own art school. (He later became the first Japanese Professor of Western-style Painting at the Tokyo School of Fine Arts.) *Lake Shore* is an ingenious fusion of late nineteenth-century French styles with the courtesan-prints popular in Japan for over a century. But here the woman is emancipated, and *ennui* is replaced by intelligence. Kuroda demonstrates a breadth of vision which is beyond the chauvinism or narrow parochialism prevalent among hidebound Japanese image-makers both then and now. For it is only when an artist has lived abroad and has fully absorbed a foreign culture that he can see his own with clarity and objectivity. The inferiority complex in face of technologically 'more advanced' nations dissolves and a true synthesis of old and new, East and West, takes place.

157 *Lake Shore* by Kuroda Seiki. Oil on canvas, Western style painting (*yōga*).
1897.

Another Meiji effort at mirror-parity was to ape the West in having
only one religion. To this end, Shintō was disentangled from foreign
Buddhism. Buddhist monasteries and art treasures were systematically
destroyed, and had it not been for the timely appointment of Dr Ernest
Fenollosa (1853–1908) as Professor of Philosophy at the Imperial
University of Tokyo, and the arrival of his wealthy Boston friend
William Bigelow, much more would have been lost. Together they
purchased the huge collection of ancient Japanese Buddhist art which
forms the core of the Asian collections in the Boston Museum of Fine
Arts. More important for Japan, perhaps, was Fenollosa's advice to the
Japanese government that indigenous artistic traditions should be pre-
served and practised – for at the time all branches of art studies, from oil
painting to industrial design, were of Western origin.

The modified traditional Japanese painting style promoted by Fenollosa was called *Nihonga*, to be distinguished from Western-style oil painting
(*Yōga*). He maintained that powerful, expressive Japanese line was

essential but that it should be reinforced with more realistic Western *chiaroscuro* and a brighter range of colours. By 1891, when Fenollosa left Japan to become director of the Oriental art department of the Boston Museum of Fine Arts, the survival of *Nihonga* painting in Japan was assured. His brilliant disciple, the philosopher Okakura Tenshin (1862–1913) became director of the Tokyo School of Fine Arts. In contrast to Fenollosa's stress on the bold Kanō-school line, Okakura promoted a delicately expressive line derived from *Yamato-e*. (Okakura often wrote and lectured in English on Japanese aesthetics and was as instrumental in promoting Japanese art abroad as he was in retaining native traditions at home.)

Traditional Japanese influences and styles in *Nihonga* painting include pure ink landscapes, colour-wash styles and thick *impasto* screens with coloured designs on gold. (Although originally painted on screens or in hanging scroll format, *Nihonga* works today are usually framed in Western style since mineral pigments are easily damaged by repeated rolling and unrolling.) Themes include standard Eastern figures and landscape compositions, as well as Western motifs and near-abstract designs; the mode is unified by the materials (writing brush, and ink or mineral pigment, on silk or paper).

Among the major artists at the turn of the century was the short-lived Hishida Shunsō (1874–1910), a student of Okakura Tenshin. (He studied in Tokyo and later taught at Tenshin's Japan Institute of Fine Arts.) His style was a new departure for that time, using no overt line-work, and was condemned by critics as being muddled or incompetent. In *Fallen Leaves*, Shunsō combines Western realism with the poetry of space: trees seem to recede into an all-pervading mist, losing definition. (There is a reference to Tōhaku's magnificent *Pine Forest* but the statement is otherwise in the language of Western realism.) 158

The giants of more typical, representative *Nihonga* are two old friends who toured Europe together in the twenties and visited China several times, Kobayashi Kokei (1883–1967) and Maeda Seison (1885–1977). Kokei encloses his forms with fine, taut lines which seem to have a life of their own. Often a subtle reverse shading from light to dark progresses from outline to centre of each form, as if the hues, startled by the line, have withdrawn in haste. Similarly, the delicate shading enveloping his motifs functions like the 'emotive cloud' and 'blush' or 'breathe' or both. A famed New York critic confessed he found *Nihonga* lifeless and dull and wondered why the Japanese love it so. This is because he was waiting for the work to arouse him. Instead, he should have 'entered' the painting quietly and receptively. Then the dramatic tension of Kokei's *Fruit* which 134

158 *Fallen Leaves* by Hishida Shunsō. Right-hand screen of double-six-fold screen; mineral pigments on paper, Japanese style painting (*Nihonga*). 1910.

electrifies the still life and charges the air, the subtle depiction of the fruit's colour, the quivering emotive space, would have transported him to the world of Japanese sensibilities which have quickened screens and scrolls for over a thousand years.

Kokei's gentle perception of the world contrasts with the vigorous vision of Maeda Seison, his lifelong friend, and instructor to the Empress till his death in 1977. Most halls in the Gosho Imperial Palace in Tokyo display a single *Nihonga* work; Seison's magnificent *Lion Dancer Awaiting Cue* (1955) enlivens the enclosing space with typical tautness. The masked and robed actor is shown at the moment of highest psychological tension, just prior to breaking into dance. Seison's works are usually highly restrained, holding in reserve formidable energies. As in *onna-e* painting, he explores the world of inner emotional turbulence beneath surface calm. The difference is that Seison's subjects are not victims of affairs of the heart but often warriors before battle, medical students at the anatomy lesson (an autopsy), women at the bath, etc. In the manner of the *Frolicking Animals* scroll, Seison once painted a long ink monochrome hand-scroll of *Monkey's Journey to the West*. He explored all major traditions, bringing a new life to each. In 1930, he even rivalled the sumptuous Kōrin, challenging his *Iris* screen with a stupendous double six-fold screen of red and white *Poppies* on a gold ground: *impasto* flowers

159

194

of the same height range across both screens in one daring, continuous horizontal band, against a flat, gold ground (white poppies in full bloom on the right screen, red poppies still in firm bud along the left screen). The relentless continuum is dramatically broken towards the end of the left screen where the field flowers have been trampled down, revealing a curved depression and – relieving the greens of the entire panel – one and a half full blooms in an outrageous red. Seison is one of very few Japanese artists ever to contrast red and green in this bold fashion and to convey a sense of continental grandeur and monumentality in his works.

In the *Nihonga* paintings of Fukuda Heichachirō (1892–1972) and Tokuoka Shinsen (1896–1972), done in traditional pigments on silk and

159 *Lion Dancer Awaiting Cue* by Maeda Seison. *Nihonga* panel for the Imperial Palace, Tokyo. 1955.

paper, the forms are rendered in a near-abstract manner, like that common in non-Japanese abstract painting; but their expression is just as much suffused with Japanese aesthetic preferences as is the work of Kuroda Seiki. Fukuda's *Virgin Snow* of 1948 is an evocative portrait of white snow-softness in a garden setting where six stepping stones are shaded in various hues. The description *yūgen*, 'mysterious and profound', has often been applied to Tokuoka Shinsen whose *Stream* of 1954 can hardly be identified without its title. In spite of their evocative mood or emotive clouds, works such as this are entirely 'modern'; even so their effect is achieved without strained mimicry of Western modernist techniques.

160

135

One of the greatest *Nihonga* artists is Higashiyama Kaii (born in 1908) whose intellectual approach brings a new dimension to this style of painting. Many of his works exploit single motifs in single colours. The mineral pigment is burned periodically to darken its hue as the work progresses. When in 1977 his murals for the Tōshōdaiji in Nara were the subject of a major exhibition in Paris, the whole room was reproduced to scale in order to show the scale and function of his panels: they were to adorn the space in which the now secret image of Ganjin is kept. The exhibition demonstrated how the arts of the Japanese present relate

161

160 *Virgin Snow* by Fukuda Heihachirō. Colours on silk, in the abstract expressionist manner. 1948.

161 (*opposite*) *Rhythm of Snow Country* by Higashiyama Kaii. *Nihonga* panel. 1963.

intimately and harmoniously to those of the past. *Nihonga* in the Seventies, however, began to turn more towards the Viennese school of fantasy: today's works are often treated as if painted in oils in a congested manner and with high colour contrast. The movement is in danger of losing its once unique potential.

Because of its unassertive qualities, *Nihonga* painting, like *kana* calligraphy, has not received the attention it deserves from the West. The print movement, however (in spite of the indifference of a government anxious to foster a Western image through conceptual art, steel and laser sculpture, etc.), has gone from strength to strength. In the Taishō era (1912–26) artists began to design, carve and pull their own prints in a 'creative print' movement (*sōsaku hanga*). Studies in black (such as black figures walking on rainy nights) reveal particular ingenuity. Kawase Hasui (1883–1957) produced landscapes where Japanese scenery is reviewed in the light of new Western realism and dramatic colouration. By contrast, Yoshida Hiroshi (1876–1950) portrayed a world of pastel sentimentality echoing that of his Western counterpart J. Walter Phillips.

The most dynamic and original master who brought Japan's new print movement to international renown was Munakata Shikō (1905–77). His irrepressible energy and *joie de vivre* were translated into vigorous, unprecedented forms. To the end of his life he worked only with woodblock, even though most of his contemporaries had switched over to the more fashionable styles of mixed-media print. Like Enkū and Hakuin, Munakata was an anomaly in his own time, the creator of a torrent of frenzied works of alarming intensity and impulse: watching him work one formed the impression that the print possessed him rather than the other way round. His 'primitive' lack of inhibition earned him the derisive – or admiring – nickname 'Jōmon Man'.

Japanese artists today form a major force in world art, and many work in international circles. (An avant-garde image, despite vigorous promotion by the establishment, lacks a genuine basis and remains an odd phenomenon within Japan. The other arts, however, rooted in long traditions, fairly burst with vitality.) The architect Tange Kenzō (b.1913) whose revolutionary stadium and surrounding village for the 1964 Olympics animates all the space around, designs all manner of buildings in many countries. Japanese architecture, in both its traditional and its

162 From *Uto no Hanga saku* by Munakata Shikō. Ink monochrome wood-block print. 1938.

163 (*opposite*) Olympic stadium in Tokyo by Tange Kenzō. Reinforced steel, concrete. 1964.

contemporary form, has made substantial contributions to modern concepts of modular construction and the inter-relation of outdoor and indoor space. Simple lines, diffused lighting and warm textures, standard attributes of Japanese buildings for centuries, are now commonplace throughout the world.

Although Japanese sculpture lagged in the doldrums since the four-teenth century, the twentieth century has already offered the world two great masters, Noguchi Isamu (b.1904) and more recently Nagare Masayuki (b. 1923). Both explore the contrast of rough stone finishes (*warehada*) and highly polished surfaces. Nagare, whose works have never been false to their Japanese roots, has been largely ignored by the establishment at home for fear of promoting antiquated standards, in spite of his growing prestige abroad. Like many Japanese artists of vision, he has suffered from the post-war frenzy to create an international face for Japan (in commerce, shipbuilding and GNP as well as in the arts) and the resulting imposition of a rather self-conscious Western standard on

164

164 *Flight* sculpture by Nagare Masayuki, made of 400 tons of Swedish granite. From Manhattan Trade Towers. c. 1970.

Japanese artists. Whether they have lived abroad or not, artists are nowadays encouraged to emulate the latest innovation seen in foreign art journals (and immediately published in local monthlies). Contemporary art in Japan has become a political commodity and its managers are usually ignorant of Japan's own distinguished history and contributions. Professor Ienaga Saburō, describing a similar situation in eighth-century Nara (where most art mirrored the Chinese), observed, 'though it was possible to import material things... it was impossible to import the *social basis for their creation* (italics mine). Consequently continental influences extended only to such matters as exterior ornamentations... They failed to generate a profound change in the ways of thinking and living...' To a large extent, this has also been true for most of the twentieth century; whenever there have been self-doubts, Japan has held up its defensive mirror to the world and displayed art forms whose genesis lay outside Japan's own socio-cultural sphere.

The recent rise in nationalism has, however, produced signs of a changing attitude and a growing awareness that Japan's own traditions are vital and valid. The younger artists, many of whom have lived abroad, have developed a new perspective and make objective use of indigenous as well as foreign traditions. (For example, many Japanese printmakers from William Hayter's Atelier 17 in Paris have returned to Japan, and now contribute many of the finest works in print exhibitions.)

The oldest art industry of all, pottery, continues to produce exciting work. Anonymous potters from regional folk kilns sell at Folk Art counters in department stores; potters like Yagi Kazuo (1919–1979) have introduced an urbane witticism to Japanese ceramics. His oeuvre is strikingly varied, ranging from glass and bronze to white and black pottery. The art of calligraphy, in a country which boasts one of the world's highest rates of literacy, has a large and active group of practitioners. Annual exhibitions include calligraphy in Chinese style, Japanese style, avant-garde style, and literary style (where instead of single or few words, entire poems or passages are inked). Avant-garde stylists have broken the legibility barrier and produce pyrotechnics in ink or lacquer on silk, paper or board. Calligraphy appears on book titles, magazine covers, film titles, names on buildings, handbag clasps, textiles, bar signs and napkins. There is hardly an aspect of contemporary Japanese

165

166

167

165 *Letter* by Yagi Kazuo. Black pottery. 28.5×41×10.5 cm. 1964.

166 *Uraurato tereru haru bi ni.* Calligraphy in *onnade* (now called *kana*) style by Kan Makiko. 1977.

167 *(below) En* (Round) by Morita Shiryū. Avant-garde calligraphy; ink on paper. 1967.

life untouched by the well-turned calligraph, be it in Chinese characters, the fluid *hiragana* or the angular *katakana* often used for foreign sounds.

Although the average Japanese today is schooled to distinguish 'fine art' (placed on museum pedestals) from applied art (in clothing, houses, pottery, garden-design or trains), he is nevertheless as susceptible to the beauty or to the sadness of things as ever. For to him all things in nature are potentially beautiful – and, if they are made by man, ought to be. For the Japanese, as for peoples of few other nations, this quality of beauty which touches them, and its expression in art, is an inseparable part of life itself.

Select Bibliography

General

René Grousset, *Les Civilizations de l'Orient*, vol IV, *Le Japon*, Paris, 1930
The Japan Foundation, *An Introductory Bibliography for Japanese Studies*
J. Edward Kidder, Jr., *Japanese Temples: Sculpture, Paintings, Gardens and Architecture*, London, 1964
Sherman E. Lee, *A History of Far Eastern Art*, New York and London, 1964
Seiroku Noma, *The Arts of Japan*, 2 vols, trans. John Rosenfield and Glenn Webb, Tokyo, 1966–67
Kakuzō Okakura, *The Ideals of the East*, London, 1920
— *The Book of Tea*, 1906, Tokyo reprint, 1956.
Robert Treat Paine and Alexander C. Soper, *The Art and Architecture of Japan*, London 1955
Robert K. Reischauer, *Early Japanese History*, 2 vols, Princeton, 1937
Laurance P. Roberts, *A Connoisseur's Guide to Japanese Museums*, Tokyo, 1967
— *A Dictionary of Japanese Artists*, Tokyo, 1976
George G. Sansom, *Japan, A Short Cultural History*, London, 1931, revised ed. London 1948
— *A History of Japan*, 3 vols, Stanford, 1958–63
Peter Swann, *A Concise History of Japanese Art*, Tokyo, 1979, revised ed. of *An Introduction to the Arts of Japan*, Oxford, 1958
Yukio Yashiro (ed.), *Art Treasures of Japan*, 2 vols, Tokyo, 1960

Early

C.M. Aikens and T. Higuchi, *Prehistory of Japan*, New York and London, 1982
Namio Egami, *The Beginnings of Japanese Art*, New York and Tokyo, 1973
J. Edward Kidder Jr., *Early Japanese Art: the Great Tombs and Treasures*, Princeton and London, 1964
— *The Birth of Japanese Art*, New York and Washington, 1965

— *Japan before Buddhism*, new ed., London, 1966
— *Prehistoric Japanese Arts: Jōmon Pottery*, Tokyo, 1968
Fumio Miki, *Haniwa*, New York and Tokyo, 1974
E.S. Morse, *Shell Mounds of Ōmori*, Memoirs of the Science Department, University of Tokyo, 1879, reprinted 1968
Robert J. Smith and Richard K. Beardsley (eds.), *Japanese Culture: Its Development and Characteristics*, Chicago, 1962

Architecture

Werner Blaser, *Japanese Temples and Tea Houses*, New York, 1956
— *Structure and Form in Japan*, New York, 1963
Y. Katsura Ishimoto, *Tradition and Creation in Japanese Architecture* (texts by Walter Gropius and Tange Kenzō), New Haven, 1960
Teiji Itō and Y. Futagawa, *The Essential Japanese House*, Tokyo, 1967
— *The Elegant Japanese House*, Tokyo, 1969
Japan Architect, English language ed. of *Shin-kenchiku* (New Architecture), monthly journal published by Shin-kenchiku-sha, Tokyo
J. Edward Kidder Jr., *Japanese Temples*, Tokyo, 1966
Harumichi Kitao, *Shoin Architecture in Detailed Illustrations*, Tokyo, 1956
Bunji Kobayashi, *Japanese Architecture*, Tokyo, 1968, revised 1970
Hirotarō Ōta, *Japanese Architecture and Gardens*, Tokyo, 1966

Ceramics

Rand Castile, *The Way of Tea*, New York and Tokyo, 1971
Louise Cort, *Shigaraki, Potters' Valley*, Tokyo, 1979
Williams Bowyer Honey, *The Ceramic Art of China and Other Countries of the Far East*, London 1948

Soame Jenyns, *Japanese Porcelain*, London, 1965
— *Japanese Pottery*, London, 1971
Fujio Koyama *The Heritage of Japanese Ceramics*, trans, and adapted by Sir John Figgess, New York and Tokyo, 1973
Bernard Leach, *A Potter in Japan*, London, 1971
Tsugio Mikami, *The Art of Japanese Ceramics*, New York and Tokyo, 1972
Roy Andrew Miller, *Japanese Ceramics*, Rutland and Tokyo, 1960
Hugo Munsterberg, *The Folk Arts of Japan*, Vermont and Tokyo, 1958
Daniel Rhodes, *Tamba Pottery*, Tokyo, 1970
Masahiko Satō, *Kyoto Ceramics*, New York and Tokyo, 1973
N. Saunders, *The World of Japanese Ceramics*, Tokyo, 1967
Joan Stanley-Baker, *Mingei: Folkcrafts of Japan*, Victoria, B.C., 1979

Gardens

Masao Hayakawa, *The Garden Art of Japan*, New York and Tokyo, 1973
— *The Garden Art of Japan*, trans. R.L. Cage, New York and Tokyo, 1974
Loraine E. Kuck, *The World of the Japanese Garden: From Chinese Origins to Modern Landscape Art*, New York and Tokyo, 1968
Osamu Mori, *Katsura Villa*, Tokyo, 1930, new ed. 1956
— *Typical Japanese Gardens*, Tokyo, 1962
— *Kobori Enshū*, Tokyo, 1974
P. and S. Rambach, *Sakuteiki ou le Livre Secret des Jardins Japonais*, Geneva, 1973
I. Schaarschmidt-Richter, *Japanische Garten*, Baden-Baden, 1977
— and Osamu Mori, *Japanese Gardens*, New York, 1979
S. Shimoyama, *Sakutei-ki, The Book of Gardens*, Tokyo, 1976

Lacquers, Textiles and Armour

Raymond Bushell, *The Inrō Handbook*, New York and Tokyo, 1979
J. Earle, *An Introduction to Netsuke*, London, 1980
Helen Benton Minnich and Nomura Shōjirō, *Japanese Costume and the Makers of its Elegant Tradition*, Vermont and Tokyo, 1963
Seiroku Noma, *Japanese Costume and Textile Arts*, New York and Tokyo, 1979

Beatrix von Ragué, *A History of Japanese Lacquer-work*, Toronto and Buffalo, 1976
W. Robinson, *Arms and Armour of Old Japan*, London, 1951
— *The Arts of the Japanese Sword*, London, 1961, 1970

Painting, Calligraphy and Prints

Terukazu Akiyama, *Japanese Painting*, Geneva, 1961, New York, 1977
Laurence Binyon and J.I.O. Sexton, *Japanese Colour Prints*, New York 1923, 2nd ed. Basil and Grey (eds.), London, 1960
James Cahill, *Scholar Painters of Japan: the Nanga School*, New York, 1972
Arthur D. Ficke, *Chats on Japanese Prints*, London, 1928, reprint Vermont and Tokyo, 1958
Jan Fontein and Money L. Hickman, *Zen Painting and Calligraphy*, Boston, 1970
Calvin, L. French, *Shiba Kokan: Artist, Innovator and Pioneer in the Westernization of Japan*, New York and Tokyo, 1974
Elise Grilli, *The Art of the Japanese Screen*, New York and Tokyo, 1970
Jack Hillier, *The Japanese Print: a New Approach*, Vermont and Tokyo, 1975
— *The Uninhibited Brush*, London, 1974
— and L. Smith, *Japanese Prints: 300 Years of Albums and Books*, London, 1980
Saburō Ienaga, *Painting in the Yamato Style*, New York and Tokyo, 1973
Hiroshi Kanazawa, *Japanese Ink Painting*, Tokyo, 1979
Richard Lane, *Masters of the Japanese Print*, London, 1962
Takaaki Matsushita, *Ink Painting*, New York and Tokyo, 1974
Kurt Meissner, *Japanese Woodblock Prints in Miniature: the Genre of Surimono*, Vermont and Tokyo, 1970
James A. Michener, *Japanese Prints: From the Early Masters to the Modern*, Vermont and Tokyo, 1959
Hiroshi Mizuo, *Edo Painting: Sōtatsu and Kōrin*, New York and Tokyo, 1972
Yūjirō Nakata, *The Art of Japanese Calligraphy*, New York and Tokyo, 1973
Yoshitomo Okamoto, *The Namban Art of Japan*, New York and Tokyo, 1972
Hideo Okudaira, *Narrative Picture Scrolls*, no. 5 in *Arts of Japan* series, New York and Tokyo, 1973
John M. Rosenfield and Fumiko and Edwin Cran-

ston, *The Courtly Tradition in Japanese Art and Literature*, Tokyo, 1973

John M. Rosenfield and Shimada Shūjirō, *Traditions of Japanese Art*, Cambridge, Mass., 1970

Jōhei Sasaki, *Ōkyo and the Maruyama-shijō School of Japanese Painting*, St Louis, 1980

Dietrich Seckel and Akihisa Hase, *Emakimono: the Art of the Japanese Painted Handscroll*, London and New York, 1959

Yoshiaki Shimizu and Carolyn Wheelwright (eds.), *Japanese Ink Paintings*, Princeton, 1976

Joan Stanley-Baker, *Nanga: Idealist Painting of Japan*, Victoria, B.C., 1980

— *The Calligraphy of Kan Makiko*, Victoria B.C., 1979

Harold P. Stern, *Master Prints of Japan: Ukiyo-e Hanga*, New York, 1969

Seiichirō Takahashi, *Traditional Woodblock Prints of Japan*, New York and Tokyo, 1972

Ichimatsu Tanaka, *Japanese Ink Painting: From Shūbun to Sesshū*, vol. 12 in *Survey of Japanese Art*, New York and Tokyo, 1972

William Watson, *Sōtatsu*, London, 1959

— *Buson*, London, 1960

Sculpture

Michiaki Kawakita, *Modern Currents in Japanese Art*, New York and Tokyo

J. Edward Kidder Jr., *Masterpieces of Japanese Sculpture*, Vermont and Tokyo, 1961

Seiichi Mizuno, *Asuka Buddhist Art: Hōryū-ji*, New York and Tokyo, 1974

Hisashi Mori, *Sculpture of the Kamakura Period*, New York and Tokyo, 1974

Tanio Nakamura, *Contemporary Japanese-style Painting*, Tokyo, 1969

Minoru Ōoka, *Temples of Nara and Their Art*, New York and Tokyo, 1973

Takaaki Sawa, *Art in Japanese Esoteric Buddhism*, New York and Tokyo, 1972

William Watson, *Sculpture of Japan*, London, 1959

Korea and Japan in the protohistoric period. (Modern cities are marked in italics.)

Japan, main districts and prefectures.

List of Illustrations

Measurements are given in centimetres followed by inches. H. = height, W. = width, L. = length and D. = diameter or depth.

1 Stepping-stones in a bed of moss in a garden.
2 *Bizen* vase. Momoyama period. Unglazed pottery. H. 25.2 (9.9) D. at mouth 8.5 (3.3). Gotō Museum, Tokyo.
3 *Kōgō* incense box in the shape of an actress. Edo period. Awaji ware with overglaze enamels on earthenware body. H. 6.5 (2.6.) W. 4.3 (1.7). Collection of the Montreal Museum of Fine Arts. Gift of Joseph-Arthur Simard.
4 *Minka* (farm-house) of the Tsubokawa family. Late 17th century. Maruoka-chō, Sakai-gun, Fukui.
5 Horned *sake* cask. 19th century. Black lacquer. H. 57.8 (22.8). Chidō Museum, Tsuruoka.
6 *Umataka* urn. Middle Jōmon period. Fired clay. H. 32 (12.6). Excavated from Niigata Prefecture. Private collection.
7 Clay figurine with crown-shaped hair and 'insect' eyes. Late Jōmon period. H. 36 (14.3) W. 22 (8.7). Excavated from the Ebisudagakoi site, Miyagi. Tōhoku University, Sendai.
8 *Nonakado* stone group in 'sundial' arrangement at centre of burial pit. Late Jōmon period. Oyū, Akita.
9 Pitcher of whitish clay showing horizontal decoration and openwork footrim. Mid Yayoi period. H. 22 (8.7) D. at mouth 9.7 (3.8). Excavated from Arazawa, Nara. Yamato Historical Museum, Nara.
10 *Dōtaku*, bronze bell. Late Yayoi period. H. 44.8 (17.6). Excavated from Kaichiyami site, Yao, Osaka. National Museum, Tokyo.
11 Aerial view of tumulus of Emperor Nintoku. Tumulus period. Overall length, including moats, 1000 metres (0.62 miles). Sakai, Osaka.
12 *Haniwa* pottery farmer. Late Tumulus period. H. 92 (36.3). Excavated from tomb at Akaborimura, Gumma. National Museum, Tokyo.
13 Wall painting of a man leading a horse. Late Tumulus period. Painted slab. W. *c.* 218.4 (86). Takehara Tomb, Wakamiya, Fukuoka.
14 Back of bronze mirror of *chokkomon* type. 5th century. H. 28 (11). From the Ōtsuka Tomb,

Shinayama, Umami in Kita-katsuragi County, Nara. National Museum, Tokyo.
15 Izumo Taisha Shintō shrine showing covered stairway and Main Sanctuary. Rebuilt 1744. 10.9 sq. metres (35.8 sq. feet). Shimane.
16 Aerial view of the Ise Jingū showing Naikū's two sectors. 4th century. Photo: Watanabe.
17 Aerial view of Hōryūji compound, pagoda to west, Golden Hall to east. Late 7th century. Ikaruga, Nara.
18 Buddhist Tiger *jātaka*, left panel from base of Tamamushi Shrine. Mid-7th century. Oil on lacquered cypress. H. 65 (25.7) W. 35.5 (14). Hōryūji, Nara.
19 Tamamushi Shrine with roof of camphor and cypress wood. Asuka period, *c.* 650. Total H. 233 (91.7). Hōryūji, Nara.
20 Tenjūkoku Mandala (detail), silk embroidery fragment. Asuka period. Chūgūji, Hōryūji, Nara.
21 Shaka Triad, Tori school. 623. Bronze Shaka Buddha H. 86.3 (34), attendants H. 91 (35.8). Golden Hall, Hōryūji, Nara.
22 Guze Kannon (detail). Early 7th century. Gilded camphor wood. H. 197 (78). Yumedono, Hōryūji, Nara.
23 Meditating Miroku Bosatsu. Early 7th century. Red pine. H. 123.5 (48.6). Kōryūji, Kyoto
24 Meditating bodhisattva (detail). Early 7th century. Wood. H. 87.5 (34.4). Chūgūji convent, Nara.
25 Zōchō Ten (Virūdhaka), one of the four Guardian Kings. Before 646. Wood. H. 20.7 (52.5). Golden Hall, Hōryūji, Nara.
26 One of six standing bodhisattvas (detail). Late 7th century. Camphor wood. H. 85.7 (33.8). Hōryūji, Nara.
27 Gakkō bodhisattva from the Yakushi Triad. 688. Gilt bronze. H. 315.3 (124). Kondō Hall, Yakushiji, Nara.
28 Amida and two attendants, a screen in Lady Tachibana's Shrine. 733. Gilt bronze. H. 33 (13). Hōryūji, Nara.

29 'Yumetagai Kannon'. Late Hakuhō period. Bronze. H. 85.7 (33.8). Hōryūji, Nara.
30 Monjū bodhisattva from Hōryūji pagoda. Tempyō period, 711. Clay. H. 50.9 (20). Hōryūji, Nara.
31 Fukūkenjaku Kannon (detail). 746. Gilded dry lacquer. H. 360.3 (141.8). Hokkedō, Tōdaiji, Nara.
32 Rushana Buddha. 759. Gilded dry lacquer. H. 303 (134). Tōshōdaiji, Nara.
33 Kannon from the Amida Paradise (detail) from the Kondō, Hōryūji. 711. Colour on plaster. Panel No. 6, H. 312 (120) W. 265 (102). Hōryūji Museum, Nara.
34 Tōdaiji scene showing the Great Buddha in the *Shigisan Engi*. 12th century. Narrative handscroll, ink and light colour wash on paper. H. 31.5 (12). Chōgosonshiji, Mt. Shigi, Nara.
35 Kondō (Golden Hall) of Tōshōdaiji. Nara period, late 8th century. H. 14.65 metres (48.4 feet). L. 28 metres (91.9 feet). Nara. Photo: Sakamoto Photo Research Laboratories.
36 Kōdō (Lecture Hall) of Tōshōdaiji. c. 748. Moved to present site in 760, remodelled in 1275 and 1675. L. 33.8 metres (110.9 feet). Nara. Photo: Sakamoto Photo Research Laboratories.
37 Ganjin (detail). Late 8th century. Dry lacquer. H. 79.7 (31.4). Kaizan dō, Tōshōdaiji, Nara.
38 Painting of entertainers on inside surface of long bow. Before 756. Ink, lacquer on catalpa wood. Overall L. 162 (63.7). Shōsōin, Tōdaiji, Nara.
39 Pair of knives. 8th century. Rhinoceros-horn hilt and silver scabbard, decorated with jewels. L. 22.9 (9). Shōsōin, Tōdaiji, Nara.
40 *Ruan Xian* (4-stringed lute). Early 7th century. Wood and inlaid mother-of-pearl. L. 100.4 (39.5) D. 39 (15.4). Shōsōin, Tōdaiji, Nara.
41 Covered medicine jar. 811. Ash-glaze on shoulders. H. 18.5 (7.3) D. 23 (9.1). Shōsōin, Tōdaiji, Nara.
42 Landscape with figures: plectrum guard of *biwa* lute. Before 756. Shitan wood decorated with marquetry. H. 38.6 (15.2) L. 17.7 (6.7). Shōsōin, Tōdaiji, Nara.
43 Map of Tōdaiji, precincts (detail). 756. Ink and light colours on hemp. H. 297 (116.9) W. 221 (87). Shōsōin, Tōdaiji, Nara.
44 Womb Mandala (detail). Heian period, 859–880. Ink and colours on silk. H. 183.3 (72.2) W. 154 (60.6). Tōji, Kyoto.
45 *Amida on a cloud*: central panel of Amida triptych. Early 11th century. Colours on silk. H. 186.7 (73.5) W. 143.4 (56.5). Hokkeji, Nara.
46 *Blue Fudō and his dōji attendants*. Mid-11th century. Colours on silk. H. 203.3 (80) W. 148.8 (58.6). Shōrenin, Kyoto.
47 Yakushi Nyorai (detail). Early 9th century.

Painted cypress wood. H. 170.3 (67). Golden Hall, Jingōji, Kyoto.
48 Shaka Nyorai. Late 9th century. Wood. H. 238 (93.7). Golden Hall, Murōji, Nara.
49 View of the Phoenix Hall, Byōdōin, Uji, Kyoto, completed in 1053.
50 *Raigō of Amida and Celestial Host* (detail) from mural in Phoenix Hall. 1053. Colours on wood. H. 75 (29.5). W. 17.5 (8.9). Byōdōin, Uji, Kyoto.
51 Celestial bodhisattva on a cloud, by the school of Jōchō. 1053. Painted wood. H. c. 50 (c. 19.7). Phoenix Hall, Byōdōin, Uji, Kyoto.
52 Buddha Amida by Jōchō. 1053. Gold leaf and lacquer on wood. H. 295 (116). Phoenix Hall, Byōdōin, Uji, Kyoto.
53 *Suiten* (Water Deva), one of twelve. 1127. Colours and gold on silk. H. 144.2 (56.8) W. 126.6 (49.8). Tōji, Kyoto.
54 *Raigō* Kannon Bosatsu. 1094. Lacquered and gilded wood. H. 96.7 (38.4). Sokujōji, Kyoto.
55 *Descent of Amida over the Mountains*. Early 13th century. Hanging scroll, colours and gold on silk. H. 138 (49) W. 118 (32). Zenrinji, Kyoto.
56 *Haya raigō* of Amida and bodhisattvas. 13th century. Hanging scroll, colours and gold on silk. H. 145.1 (57.1) W. 154.5 (60.8). Chionin, Kyoto.
57 *Early Spring Landscape,* door panel in Phoenix Hall. 1053. Painted wood. H. 374.5 (147.4) W. 138.6 (54.6). Byōdōin, Kyoto.
58 *Kashiwagi I*, detail from *The Tale of Genji*. Early 12th century. Handscroll, ink and colours on paper. H. 21.8 (8.6) W. 48.3 (19). Tokugawa Collection, Nagoya.
59 *Ban Dainagon E-kotoba,* second of three scrolls. Late 12th century. Ink and colours on paper. Sakai Collection, Tokyo.
60 *Simian Prelate worshipping Frog Buddha* from the *Chōjū Giga* scroll I. Late 12th century. Ink on paper. H. 31 (12.2). Kōzanji Collection, Kyoto.
61 *Hungry Ghosts wait to feast on Feces* from the *Gaki Zōshi* scroll (Kawamoto version). Late 12th century. Ink and colours on paper. H. 27.3 (10.7). National Museum, Tokyo.
62 Enichi-bō Jōnin, *Myōe meditating*. Early 13th century. Hanging scroll, ink and colours on paper. H. 145 (57) W. 48.8 (19.2). Kōzanji Collection, Kyoto.
63 *Burning of the Sanjō Palace*. Detail from the *Heiji monogatari* handscroll I. Late 13th century. Ink and colours on paper. H. 41.3 (16.3) W. 699.7 (275.4). Courtesy, Museum of Fine Arts, Boston. Fenollosa-Weld Collection.
64 *Suzumushi II*, detail from *The Tale of Genji* handscrolls. Early 12th century. Ink and colour on paper. H. 21.8 (8.6) W. 48.2 (19). Gotō Museum, Tokyo.

65 Yakuō Bosatsu Honjibon. Frontispiece to the 23rd scroll of the *Heike Nōgyō. c.* 1164. Colours and *kirigane* on paper. Itsukushima Shrine, Hiroshima.

66 *The Flying Granary,* detail from the first *Shigisan Engi* handscroll. *c.* 1156–1180. Ink and colours on paper. H. 31.5 (12.4). Chōgosonshiji, Mt. Shigi, Nara.

67 Enichi-bō Jōnin, *Zemmyō transformed into a Dragon,* detail from the *Kegon Engi* handscrolls. Early 13th century. Ink and colours on paper. H. 31.6 (12.4). Kōzanji, Kyoto.

68 *Onnade* calligraphy of Kiyohara Fukayabu from one of the *Masu-shikishi* set of calligraphies ascribed to Fujiwara no Yukinari. Late 11th century. Album leaf mounted as *shikishi.* Ink on paper. H. 13.8 (5.4) W. 11.8 (4.7). Private collection, Japan.

69 Calligraphy fragment from the *Shigeyukishū* collection from the *Sanjūrokunin ka shū, c.* 1112. Ink on decorated paper. H. 20.1 (7.9) W. 31.8 (12.5). Nishi Honganji, Kyoto.

70 *So* (horizontal harp) with flowing stream and small birds. 12th century. Lacquered wood with *maki-e.* L. 151.9 (59.8). Kasuga-Taisha Shintō Shrine, Hiroshima.

71 Armour with blue yarns from the Taira clan. 12th century. H. 39.5 (15.6). Itsukushima Shrine, Hiroshima.

72 Unkei (d. 1223), *Muchaku.* 1208–12. Painted wood. H. 188 (74). Kōfukuji, Nara.

73 *Furuna,* one of *Ten Great Disciples.* Nara period, *c.* 734. Painted dry lacquer. H. 149 (58.7). Kōfukuji, Nara.

74 Tankei (1173?–1256), *Basū-sen* (detail). Early 13th century. Polychrome painted wood. H. 154.7 (60.9). Myōhō-in, Kyoto.

75 Tankei (1173?–1256), *Mawara-nyō* (detail). Early 13th century. Polychrome painted wood. H. 153.7 (60.5). Myōhō-in, Kyoto.

76 Lanqi Daolong (1213–1278) (detail). 1271. Hanging scroll, ink and colours on silk. H. 104.8 (41.3) W. 46.4 (18.3). Kenchōji, Kamakura.

77 Fujiwara Takanobu (1142–1205), *The Shōgun Minamoto no Yoritomo.* Hanging scroll, ink and colours on silk. H. 139.4 (54) W. 111.8 (44). Jingoji, Kyoto.

78 Goshin (active 1334–49), the Emperor *Hanazono.* 1338. Hanging scroll, ink and colours on paper. H. 31.2 (12.9) W. 97.3 (38.3). Chōfukuji, Kyoto.

79 Mokuan Reien (d. 1345), *Four Sleepers.* Inscription by Xiangfu Shaomi. Hanging scroll, ink on paper. H. 73.4 (28.9) W. 32.4 (12.8). The Maeda Ikutokukai Collection, Tokyo.

80 Gyokuen Bompō (*c.* 1347–*c.* 1420), *Orchids and Rocks.* Hanging scroll, ink on paper. H. 106.5 (39.5) W. 34.5 (13.1). Metropolitan Museum of Art, The Harry G. C. Packard Collection of Asian Art.

81 Kinkakuji (Golden Pavilion), Kyoto, 1398. Original destroyed by fire in 1950 and rebuilt in 1964.

82 Gukei (active 1361–75), *White-robed Kannon with Flanking Landscapes.* Hanging scrolls, ink on silk. H. 98.6 (38.8) W. 40.3 (15.9) each. *White-robed Kannon* in Yamato Bunkakan Collection, Nara. *Landscapes* in Masuda Collection, Kyoto.

83 Ryōzen (active mid-14th century), *White Heron.* Hanging scroll, ink on paper. H. 35.1 (13.9) W. 32 (12.6). Nagatake Asano Collection.

84 Penglai, the immortals' isle, arrangement of seven rocks in the pond garden of Tenryūji, Kyoto, completed by 1265.

85 Josetsu (active early 15th century), *Catching Catfish with a Gourd.* 1408. Hanging scroll, ink and colours on paper with inscriptions by thirty monks. H. 111.5 (43.9) W. 76 (29.9). Taizōin, Kyoto.

86 Shūbun (active 1423–60), *Reading in the Bamboo Studio* (detail). Mid-15th century. Hanging scroll, ink on paper. H. 134.8 (53) W. 33.3 (13). National Museum, Tokyo.

87 Shōkei Tenyū (active 1436–65), *Small Lake Landscape.* Hanging scroll, ink and colours on paper. H. 121.5 (47.8) W. 34.8 (13.7). Fujii Collection, Hyōgo.

88 *Reading in the Bamboo Studio* (whole). See 86.

89 Bunsei (active 1460s), *West Lake,* inscribed by Zuikei Shūhō and Ichijō Kanera. Before 1473. Hanging scroll, ink on paper. H. 80.8 (31.8) W. 33.4 (13.1). Masaki Art Museum, Osaka.

90 Sōami (d. 1525), *Eight Views of the Xiao and Xiang,* detail of one of the 23 sliding door panels. 1509. Ink on paper. H. 174.8 (68.8) W. 140.2 (55.2). Daisen-in, Daitokuji, Kyoto.

91 Bokusai (d. 1492), *Ikkyū Sōjun.* Before 1481. Hanging scroll, ink and colours on paper. H. 46 (17) W. 26.5 (10). National Museum, Tokyo.

92 Sesshū Tōyō (1420–1506), *Landscape* (detail), inscribed by Ryōan Keigo in 1507. Hanging scroll, ink and light colours on paper. H. 119 (46.9) W. 35.3 (13.9). Ohara Kenichirō Collection, Osaka.

93 Sōen (active 1489–1500), *Haboku* landscape. Late 15th or early 16th century. Ink on paper. Andō Collection, Tokyo.

94 Tōshun (active first half of the 15th century), *Evening Snow* from *Eight Views of the Xiao and Xiang.* Hanging scroll, ink on paper. H. 22 (8.7) W. 31.7 (12.5). Masaki Art Museum, Osaka.

95 Sesson Shūkei (*c.* 1504–89), *Hawk on Pine.* Mid-16th century. One of pair of hanging scrolls, ink on paper. H. 126.5 (49.9) W. 53.6 (21.1). National Museum, Tokyo.

96 Sesson Shūkei (*c.* 1504–89), *Landscape in Wind.*

Hanging scroll, ink on paper. H. 27.3 (10.8) W. 78.6 (18.8) (painting only). Sansō Collection, U.S.A.

97 Dry landscape garden in Ryōanji, Kyoto, constructed in the 1480s. Japan Tourist Organisation.

98 Kanō Eitoku (1543–1590), *Pine and Crane.* 1566. Sliding door panels, ink on paper. H. 176 (69.3). Jukōin, Daitokuji, Kyoto.

99 Himeji castle, Hyōgo Prefecture, built late 16th century.

100 *Great Pine* murals in the Great Hall of Ninomaru Goten, attributed to Kanō Tanyū (1602–74). 1624–26. Ink and colours on gold-foiled paper panels. Nijō Castle, Kyoto.

101 Kanō Sanraku (1559–1635), *White Peonies* (detail). Early 17th century. Sliding door panel, colours and *impasto* on gold foil. H. 184.5 (72.6) W. 99 (40). Daitokuji, Kyoto.

102 Kanō Tanyū (1602–74), *Night Fishing with Cormorants.* Mid-17th century. A six-fold screen in ink, colours and gold. Okura Bunkazaidan, Tokyo.

103 Tosa school, *Landscape with Sun and Moon* (detail). Mid-16th century. Panels 2–5 of the right-hand screen. Double six-fold screen, ink, colours and gold on paper. Each H. 147 (57.8) W. 316 (124.4). Kongōji, Osaka.

104 (*left*), **105** (*right*) Kaihō Yūshō (1533–1615), *Pine and Plum by Moonlight.* Late 16th century. A pair of six-panel screens, ink and slight colour on paper. Each H. 169 (66.5) W. 353 (139). Collection, Atkins Museum of Fine Art, Kansas City, U.S.A.

106 (*left*), **107** (*right*) Hasegawa Tōhaku (1539–1610), *Pine Forest.* Late 16th century. A pair of six-panel screens, ink on paper. Each H. 156 (61.4) W. 347 (136.6). National Museum, Tokyo.

108 (*left*), **109** (*right*) Tawaraya Sōtatsu (active 1602–40?), *Matsushima (Pine Island).* Early 17th century. Double six-fold screen, ink, colours and gold on paper. H. 166 (59.8) W. 367.7 (141.3). Freer Gallery of Art, The Smithsonian Institution, Washington D.C.

110 Tanaka Chōjirō (1516–92), *Katsujishi, raku* ware tea-bowl. 16th century. Black slip glaze. H. 8.8 (3.5) Diam. 10.9 (4.3). Mingei-kan Folk-craft Museum, Kyoto.

111 (*exterior*), **112** (*interior*) Sen no Rikyū (1521–91), *Myōkian,* tea house. 1582. Myōkian, Kyoto.

113 Yōmei-mon (Sunlight Gate), Tōshōgū. Early 17th century. Nikkō, Tochigi. Japan Tourist Organisation.

114 *Katsura,* detached imperial villa and garden. 1642. Tochigi.

115 *Portuguese Missionaries and Traders arriving in Japan.* c. 1600. *Namban* (southern barbarians)

folding screen, ink, colours and gold on paper. H. 157.5 (62) W. 367 (144.5). Victoria and Albert Museum, London.

116 Small dish in *nezumi* Shino glaze with white slip painting of wagtail on rock. Momoyama period, 16th–17th century. H. 8.9 (3.5) D. 26.8 (10.6). Agency for Cultural Affairs, Tokyo.

117 *Kōgan* (Ancient Shore) water-jar in Shino ware. Momoyama period, 16th–17th century. H. 17.5 (6.9) D. 19.2 (7.6). Hatakeyama Kinen-kan Museum, Tokyo.

118 *Yabure-Bukuro* (Torn Pouch) water-jar, Iga ware. Momoyama period, late 16th, early 17th century. Stoneware. H. 21.6 (8.5) D. of rim 15.8 (6.2). Gotō Museum, Tokyo.

119 Ogata Kenzan (1663–1743), five small plates. Edo period, early 18th century. White slip and rust glaze, decorated with grey and gold pigment. Each H. 2.4 (0.9) D. 11 (4.3). Nezu Institute of Fine Arts, Tokyo.

120 Nabeshima ware plate with design of flowering buckwheat. Early 19th century. Overglaze enamels on porcelain. H. 9.1 (3.6) D. 30 (11.8).

121 Old Imari ware *sake* bottle depicting Europeans. Edo period, 17th century. Porcelain. H. 56 (22). The Cleveland Museum of Art, Gift of Ralph King.

122 Lacquered wooden chest with floral inlay of mother-of-pearl and metal, ivory handles. Early 17th century. H. 30.5 (12) W. 42.6 (16.8) D. 26.7 (10.5). Victoria and Albert Museum, London.

123 (*left*), **124** (*right*) Ogata Kōrin (1658–1716), *Irises.* Early 18th century. Double six-fold screen, colours on gold foil over paper. Each H. 151.2 (59.5) W. 360.7 (142). Nezu Art Museum, Tokyo.

125 Hon'ami Kōetsu (1558–1637), *Boat Bridge,* writing-box. Early 17th century. Inkstone case, lead and mother-of-pearl on gold lacquer. H. 11.8 (4.6) W. 24.2 (9.5) D. 22.7 (8.9). National Museum, Tokyo.

126 *Waves and Wheel of Life* lacquer handbox. Heian period, 12th century. Gold and mother-of-pearl inlay. H. 13 (5.1) W. 22.5 (8.9) L. 30.5 (12). National Museum, Tokyo.

127 Hon'ami Kōetsu (1558–1637), *Fujisan* (Mt. Fuji), *raku* ware tea-bowl. Momoyama period, early 17th century. D. 11.6 (4.6). Sakai Tadamasa Collection, Tokyo.

128 Furuta Oribe (1543–1615), *Kuro Oribe Chawan,* tea-bowl. Momoyama period, late 16th, early 17th century. H. 8.5 (3.4) D. 15 (5.9). Umezawa Memorial Museum, Tokyo.

129 Hon'ami Kōetsu (1558–1637) (calligraphy) and Tawaraya Sōtatsu (1602–40?) (painting), *Flowers and Grasses of the Four Seasons* (detail). Momoyama period, early 17th century. Poem handscroll, ink, silver and gold on paper. H. 33.7

(13.3) W. 924.1 (363.8). Hatakeyama Kinenkan Museum, Tokyo.

130 Ogata Kōrin, *Flowers and Grasses. c.* 1705. Framed handscroll, ink, colours and white pigment on paper. H. 36 (14.2) W. 131 (51.6). Private collection.

131 Yosa Buson (1716–83), *Pine Tree at Karasaki.* Detail with *Weatherworn Traveller.* 1778. Handscroll now mounted on six-fold screen, ink and colours on paper. Hamaguchi Gihei Collection, Chiba.

132 Tawaraya Sōtatsu (active 1602–40?), *Lotus and Swimming Birds.* Early 17th century. Hanging scroll, ink on paper. H. 116.5 (45) W. 50.3 (20). National Museum, Kyoto.

133 Ogata Kenzan (1663–1743), *Waterfall,* teabowl. Early 18th century. White slip glaze and rust painting. H. 8 (3.2) D. 10.3 (4.1). Private collection.

134 Kobayashi Kokei (1883–1957), *Fruit.* Early 20th century. Hanging scroll, mineral pigments on paper. Yamatane Museum of Art, Tokyo.

135 Tokuoka Shinsen (1896–1972), *Stream.* 1954. Colours on paper. H. 133.4 (52.5) W. 177.3 (69.8). Private collection.

136 Inkstone box with *yatsu hashi* design by Ogata Kōrin (1658–1716). Edo period, 18th century. H. 14.2 (5.6) L. 27.4 (10.8) W. 19.7 (7.8). National Museum, Tokyo.

137 Peacock *kosode* (short-sleeved robe) (detail). Edo period. Gold thread repoussée and embroidery.

138 *Hawk and Dragon,* courtesan's *kosode.* Edo period, early 19th century. Gold and lamé on black velvet. National Museum, Tokyo.

139 *Rooster and Flowering Tree.* Meiji period, late 19th century. Cotton panel, probably a bedcover, resist-dyed on an indigo ground, mounted as a double screen. H. 146 (57.5) W. 125 (49.2). Collection of the Art Gallery of Greater Victoria, Canada.

140 Ikeno Taiga (1723–76), *Pine Tree and Waves. c.* 1765–70s. One of double six-panel screen, light colours on paper. H. 58.5 (23) W. 118.9 (46.8).

141 Yosa Buson (1716–83), *Sumō Wrestling,* inscribed with *haiku* verses by Buson. Mid-18th century. Hanging scroll, ink and light colours on paper. H. 261 (102.8) W. 22.8 (9). Private collection, Japan.

142 Uragami Gyokudō (1745–1820), *High Winds and Banking Geese.* Album leaf from *Kokin Yojijō.* Ink and light colours on paper. H. 31 (12.2) W. 25 (9.8). Takemoto Collection, Aichi.

143 Aoki Mokubei (1767–1833), *Birthday Felicitations.* 1830. Hanging scroll, ink and light colours on satin. H. 17 (6.7) W. 23.5 (9.3). Setsu Collection, Kanagawa.

144 Maruyama Ōkyō (1733–95), *Sketches of Cicadas* (detail) from *Sketchbook of Insects.* Mid-19th century. Ink and light colours on paper. Size of sketchbook H. 26.7 (10.5) W. 19.4 (7.6). National Museum, Tokyo.

145 Nagasawa Rosetsu (1754–99), *The Itsukushima Shrine,* fifth view of *Eight Views of Miyajima* (Hiroshima). 1794. Album leaf, ink and colours on silk. H. 34.5 (13.6) W. 46.5 (18.3). Yasuda Chūzō Collection, Hiroshima.

146 Itō Jakuchū (1716–1800), *Phoenix and White Elephant.* Mid-18th century. One of pair of six-fold screens, ink and colour *impasto* on paper. H. 176 (69.3) W. 376 (148). National Museum, Tokyo.

147 Gibon Sengai (1750–1837), *Frog and Snail.* Early 19th century. Hanging scroll, ink on paper. H. 35.1 (13.8) W. 52.7 (20.7). Sansō Collection, California.

148 Enkū (1628–95), *Shō Kannon Bosatsu.* Late 17th century. Unpainted wood. H. 157.1 (61.9). Seihōji, Gifu.

149 Hakuin Ekaku (1685–1768), *Daruma* (Bodhidharma). 1751. Hanging scroll, ink on paper. H. 222.8 (87.7) W. 36.5 (14.3). Shōjūji, Aichi.

150 *Shijō-Kawara* (detail). Early 17th century. One of pair of bi-fold screens, colours on gold paper. H. 152.2 (59.9) W. 157.2 (61.9). Seikadō Collection, Tokyo.

151 Kanō Naganobu (1577–1654), *Dancing under the Cherry Trees* (detail). Early 17th century. One of pair of six-fold screens, colours on paper. H. 149 (58.7) W. 348 (137). National Museum, Tokyo.

152 Suzuki Harunobu (1724–70), *Viewing Maple Leaves by the Waterfall.* Late 1760s. 'Brocade print' (*chūban nishiki-e*). H. 27.6 (10.9) W. 20.4 (8).

153 Kitagawa Utamaro (1754–1806), *The Coquettish Type* from the series *Ten Physiognomic Types of Women.* Early 1790s. Double woodblock print. H. 37.9 (14.9) W. 24.4 (9.6).

154 Sharaku (active 1794–95), *Sakata Hangorō III as the Villain Mizuyemon,* from *Hana-ayame Bunroku Soga.* 1794. Polychrome woodblock print, with a mica-dusted background. Art Institute of Chicago.

155 Katsushika Hokusai (1760–1849), *View on a Fine Breezy Day,* from *Thirty-Six Views of Mount Fuji,* 1822–32. Polychrome woodblock print. H. 25.5 (10) L. 38 (15). Sekai-kyūsei-kyō Collection, Atami Museum, Shizuoka.

156 Andō Hiroshige (1797–1858), *Snow at Kambara* from *Fifty-Three Stations of the Tokaido.* 1833. Polychrome woodblock print. H. 24.2 (9.5) W. 36.7 (14.5).

157 Kuroda Seiki (1866–1924), *Lake Shore.* 1897.

Oil on canvas. H. 68 (26.8) L. 83.3 (32.8). National Institute of Art Research, Tokyo.
158 Hishida Shunsō (1874–1910), *Fallen Leaves.* Right-hand screen of double six-fold pair, colours on paper. Each H. 156.2 (61.5) W. 365 (143.8). Courtesy of the Eiseibunko Museum, Tokyo.
159 Maeda Seison (1885–1977), *Lion Dancer Awaiting Cue.* 1955. Painting inlaid in wall, mineral pigments on gold foiled paper. H. 159.5 (62.8) W. 201.5 (79.3). Hall of the Lion Dance, Imperial Palace Collection, Tokyo.
160 Fukuda Heihachirō (1892–1972), *Virgin Snow.* 1948. Colours on silk. H. 113 (44.5) W. 81.9 (32.3). Private collection.
161 Higashiyama Kaii (b. 1908), *Rhythm of Snow Country.* 1963. Colour on paper. H. 156.2 (61.5) L. 213 (84). National Theatre, Tokyo.
162 Munakata Shikō (1908–75), *The Visit* from

Uto no Hanga saku. 1938. Ink monochrome woodblock print. H. 25.4 (10) W. 28.7 (11.3).
163 Olympic stadium in Tokyo, designed by Tange Kenzō (b. 1913). 1964. Reinforced steel, concrete.
164 Nagare Masayuki (b. 1923), *Flight.* 1970. 400 tons of black Swedish granite. World Trade Centre, New York. Photo courtesy of Bank of America.
165 Yagi Kazuō (1919–1979), *Letter.* 1964. Black burnished clay. H. 28.5 (11.2) L. 41 (16) W. 10.5 (4.1).
166 Kan Makiko (b. 1933), *Uraurato tereru haru bi ni.* 1977. Hanging scroll, ink on coloured and speckled *ryōshi* paper. H. 37 (14.6) W. 33 (13). Collection the author.
167 Morita Shiryū (b. 1912), *En* (Round). 1967. Ink on paper H. 69 (27.2) W. 91 (35.8). Private Collection, Japan.

Index